PRAISE FOR
UNSTOP...

D1309997

"With Kelly as our Coach we grew by over $1,000,000 dollars in revenue this year. UNSTOPPABLE is the playbook for how to create massive leverage, rapid growth and lasting, sustainable success. There is no excuse to not invest an hour in reading UNSTOPPABLE to create a better future and achieve your goals."

-Salim Mavany,
CEO Majestic Spice

"Kelly has laid out beautifully not just the mindset behind becoming unstoppable, but she's also provided key questions, some tough love, and several thoughtful exercises throughout to help her reader breakthrough the fears, doubts and misconceptions that tend to hold us back from achieving true freedom. If you're ready to make a lasting change in your life and become unstoppable, then this book is definitely for you!"

-Kate Erickson,
EOFire

"Kelly Roach is the Game Changer. If you want to cut through the noise and get the step-by-step playbook to skyrocket your business, UNSTOPPABLE, is an absolute necessity. Kelly Roach gives you the blueprint to 6 and 7 figure success and will escalate your business to the level only others dream about."

-Dr. Angela Tran,
D.O., CEO and Medical Director of Med-Fit Medical Weight Loss

"I know my life changed when Kelly started coaching me! I never imagined I would be delegating so well and learn to balance. I actually have a life and our income has doubled... It's amazing! No more 14 hour days, 6 days a week. Unstoppable is the book we all wish we had when we were starting our careers. Kelly not only nails the critical components of any successful business venture but this book makes you re-think everything in your life, challenging you to rise up and be a better version of yourself."

-Kim Phelan,
Vice President, Coalition for Hemophilia B

"UNSTOPPABLE is a must read for anyone wanting to take their business, life, and motivation to the next level. The author, Kelly Roach, speaks from remarkable experience with such powerful wisdom, confidence and pride which keeps you enthralled from the very beginning. Some business related books can get boring but this on the contrary, is a can not put down, easy to read book on how to become extremely successful from an inspiring, knowledgeable, proven business mentor!"

-Ashley Mednick,
Corporate Recruiter at Pfizer

"UNSTOPPABLE is a timeless book filled with actionable strategies, key mindset shifts and insights that anyone can apply at any stage of life. This book gives you the play by play on how to make your goals a reality. Kelly goes above and beyond sharing information you pay thousands to get elsewhere. A must read for anyone who craves more freedom, fulfillment and success in their life."

-Samantha Kelley,
Adjunct Professor, University of Delaware

"Kelly is an entrepreneur who has been through the trenches and come out on top. She's built a successful business that positively impacts the lives of thousands of people around the world, and she's designed a great lifestyle in the process. In this book, she does a fantastic job of revealing the principles and strategies that will help you make the same thing happen for you."

-Tyler Basu,
Publisher & Editor of Lifestyle Business Magazine

"Kelly Roach inspires us to live life fully, on our own terms, period. UNSTOPPABLE gives the roadmap, strategies and mindset needed to achieve extraordinary success and in record time."

-Rubina Cohen,
Success + Marketing Coach, LiveInYourGenius.com

"There are very few people with the results, expertise and experience that could deliver such a powerful and succinct roadmap for achieving unparallelled success in every facet of life. UNSTOPPABLE is a book that belongs on EVERY aspiring entrepreneur and current business owner's bookshelf. Hands down...if you want more freedom, a higher level of success, and to one day be financially free, this is a must read."

-Steve Washkalavitch
CEO, Global Loss Solutions

"Kelly Roach nails it. We have all been victims of self sabotage. She calls us on the carpet and asks us to face up to what is holding us back – us. Her new book encapsulates the "you are worthy" sentiment and helps us to believe."

-J. Kanan Sawyer,
Ph.D. (Eastern Communication President, Owner Kanan Communication,
Associate Professor at West Chester University of PA)

"Kelly Roach's smart, frank, and honest take on how to achieve success will upend your expectations and help you work and live smarter."

- Dorie Clark,
author of Stand Out and Reinventing You, and adjunct professor, Duke University's Fuqua School of Business

"UNSTOPPABLE was like Kelly herself, direct, value added and energetic. I was excited to pick it up!"

-Paul Isenberg,
CEO Bringing Hope Home

UNSTOPPABLE

NINE PRINCIPLES
FOR UNLIMITED
— SUCCESS —
IN BUSINESS AND IN LIFE

KELLY ROACH

BUSINESS GROWTH STRATEGIST | SPEAKER | PEAK PERFORMANCE COACH

UNSTOPPABLE

Nine Principles for Unlimited Success in Business and in Life

*Dedicated to Billy – my husband,
best friend, and confidant.
Without your love and support,
this book would not be possible.*

ABOUT KELLY ROACH

Kelly Roach is known internationally as an "Authority for Entrepreneurs and Business Leaders who want more success, freedom, and fulfillment in their lives." She is on a mission to help more than 1,000,000 people achieve their goals and dreams.

She has already directly helped countless individuals master sales, marketing, and business growth strategies to increase their incomes and achieve their goals.

Kelly started her career with a Fortune 500 firm where she was promoted seven times in eight years, becoming the youngest Senior Vice President in the firm. Kelly's experience hiring, training, coaching, and managing individuals across 17 locations up and down the East Coast prepared her for her entrepreneurial journey.

After breaking every record in the company's history for profit, growth, sales, and expansion, coupled with millions in profit added to the bottom line, Kelly knew it was time to focus on helping others do the same.

Kelly's number one passion in life is helping others succeed with the right strategies, action plan, and mindset for success. Kelly's company, **Kelly Roach Coaching** helps entrepreneurs, business owners and executive leaders achieve rapid, sustainable business growth in record time.

Kelly does private consulting with corporations, runs online training and coaching programs for entrepreneurs, and hosts her own Elite Mastermind for individuals who are seriously committed to transformative results in their business and life.

To learn how you can work with Kelly and her team, email coaching@kellyroachcoaching.com or visit www.kellyroachcoaching.com to connect with us today.

FREE BOOK GUIDE

This book is meant to inspire you, but it's much more than that. It is my mission to get you into action so that you can take your life to the next level. I want YOU to become "unstoppable."

To help you, there is a 100% free guide that goes along with this book that will help you get absolute clarity on where you're headed and how you can achieve your personal and business dreams.

Download the free resources by visiting:

<u>KellyRoachCoaching.com/guide</u>

TABLE OF CONTENTS

INTRODUCTION

Life is tough, no doubt about it. There are ups and downs, personal crises, family issues, health setbacks, and the list goes on. As I always say, there is a reason to be depressed each and every day... but who wants to live that way?

No matter how challenging life is, each day is a gift and a new opportunity to be the best you can be in everything you do. This is the mantra I live by. And this is why I've written this book: To help you understand that with the right mindset, strategy and actions you can achieve everything that you want and live the life you may only think is possible in your dreams. I am here to tell you it is entirely possible! I'm only one of many entrepreneurs, athletes, and artists who overcame many challenges to reach success and you can, too.

It truly does not matter where you are starting from or how far in the distant future your dream may be (or feel). If you commit with your whole being to change your life and make your dreams a reality, they *will* happen.

When I say it doesn't matter where you are now, I also mean that it doesn't matter how old you are! There are countless examples of entrepreneurs who started late in life, or began second careers after retiring from their original professions, and achieved great things and enjoyed incredible success. If you're 40 now and believe it may take five to ten years to achieve what you want, so what?

> ***It is never too late to start to dream big and achieve amazing success:***
>
> – *Julia Child was 39 before she published her first cookbook, after working in advertising and media. Her TV debut came at age 51.*
>
> – *Ray Kroc bought McDonalds in 1954 at age 52.*
>
> – *Laura Ingalls Wilder was 65 before she published the first of the "Little House" books.*
>
> – *Colonel Sanders franchised Kentucky Fried Chicken when he was 62, and sold it for $2 million 12 years later.*
>
> – *The first true Wal-Mart opened when Sam Walton was 44.*
>
> – *Henry Ford didn't launch the Ford Motor company until he was 40.*

The sections in the book reflect the three core areas you need to make your dreams a reality and how to go about achieving them:

1. Financial Abundance
2. Freedom
3. Unstoppable Success

The first two are pretty self-explanatory, and we'll cover what you need to do to achieve them. Money (aka financial abundance) isn't everything, but it does help you eliminate controllable challenges. And you're about to discover that freedom isn't free. You will be sacrificing in the short term for long-term gains.

You will also discover in reading these sections that achieving financial abundance and freedom in your life are as much about your mindset as they are about the actions you take.

The portion of the book dedicated to creating unstoppable success focuses on your personal values, the rituals you live by, the principles you embody, and a few key skills that will allow you to achieve rapid success in pretty much any situation.

Discipline and mental strength have more to do with achieving the three core areas I focus on than anything else. This is not a "feel good" book about convincing yourself to be happy in a situation in which you are not or by repeating something over and over until you believe it to be true. What it is about is splashing some cold water on your face, looking in the mirror, and realizing you – and only you – hold they keys to the kingdom. Every day you wake up and make a decision to be living or dying, progressing or staying right where you are. In the age of the Internet, there are so many free resources at our fingertips that it seems silly for anyone to say they don't have the knowledge, information, or resources to do just about anything. Where there is a will, there is always a way.

Your attitude toward yourself and others will play a "make or break" role in your ability to not just achieve high levels of success but sustain it over the course of your lifetime. As a part of your journey progressing through this book, I encourage you to check in on your perceptions, judgments, thoughts, and feelings about yourself as well as those who have achieved what you would like to achieve.

Many times, those deep-seated thoughts and feelings prevent you from taking action on the very things that will change your life for the better. Being honest with yourself about where you are and accepting total accountability for it is the only way to begin the journey to becoming the person you know deep down you are capable of being.

I came from financial struggle and grew up with a lot of stress and anxiety about money (some embarrassment, too). Growing up the way I did, I never would have guessed the immense amount of financial abundance that has flowed into and through my life would ever come to be. What I can tell you for certain is that I had a choice to make at a young age about what my future would look like and that choice came down to one thing: Settle for what I was given or go out and work as hard and for as long as it took to create the life I wanted and deserved.

I thank God every day for the blessings in my life, one being the daily financial struggle we faced that forced me to embody a fierce work ethic and determination that most people will never find the will to live out long enough to make their dreams come true. I assure you, there is almost certainly a parallel in your life – something you thought was a detriment (like financial struggle) that in reality is a blessing in your life today.

> *Making your dreams come true is largely a result of a single decision: to take daily, intentional ACTION.*

The more experience I gain as a leader, business owner, and human being, the more I feel not just the pull but also the obligation to give back. One of the most powerful messages you can take away from this book is that the challenges you have faced or are facing are building your muscle. You are exercising your brain's and body's ability to work through complex challenges and difficult situations. Many people look at where they are and it seems unimaginable that in one year their whole life can change.

It happens all the time. When you decide that you have had enough and you will give every ounce of your will, commitment, focus, and power to creating a new and different result, the guaranteed outcome is that your life will be transformed. Be open to the possibility. Dream a new dream and be willing to do the work to make it happen.

I am writing this book to give you the roadmap that I have followed and am now helping hundreds of others to follow to change their lives, their financial situations, and finally capture the freedom they are craving in their everyday lives.

It's easy to get lost in this life. Sometimes life beats you down, but you have to bounce back. We all have the ability to come back better, stronger, and capable of more. In order to grow, we have to work through challenges, setbacks, unexpected twists and turns because that is how we build our human strength. When you begin to see it in this way, your ability to overcome these things faster and with less emotional and spiritual toll improves, and you begin to unleash your truly miraculous human potential.

Pretty much everyone I come in contact with – clients, colleagues, friends and family – all want the same thing: peace of mind, stability, health, wealth, and most importantly happiness. My business and my life are committed to helping others achieve the three cores: Financial Abundance, Freedom, and Fulfillment, and my goal in writing this book is to give you the strategies to achieve all three for yourself!

Financial Abundance

There are somethings in life we can control and other things we cannot. I decided at a very young age that I would be wealthy. I knew that having financial abundance would eliminate certain problems and challenges that are 100 percent within our control versus other uncontrollables (e.g. unpreventable health issues, the death of a loved one, etc.). This decision has driven my thoughts, decisions, and behavior for many years and has created opportunity, enjoyment, and happiness in my life. No, money isn't everything, not even close, but it opens doors and makes life a whole lot more comfortable, to say the least.

Freedom

The section of the book that focuses on freedom covers the types of decisions you will have to make to create more freedom in your life. What most people don't realize is that freedom is intentionally created over a period of years through a series of strategic decisions. A huge part of creating freedom is the short-term sacrifice that creates a lifetime of reward. Most only see the sacrifice and aren't willing to do what is necessary to achieve the ultimate result. The process of creating freedom is very confusing and deters most because you actually get *less* freedom many times before you get *more*. Because you are not getting instant gratification or immediate positive reinforcement, many times – if you don't have a truly long-range vision for your life – you will give up long before you reap the benefits and rewards.

Hopefully, you are one of few who sees the incredible joy that awaits you if you are disciplined, focused, and persistent with your goals. I promise you: It is all worth it... times a million.

Fulfillment: Unstoppable Success

It was not until I got into my late twenties that I understood that wealth and success without freedom and fulfillment was poverty (and misery, I might add), and so my life took a sharp turn toward entrepreneurship. It led me to unstoppable success. You will find that the portion of the book that focuses on financial freedom covers multiple streams of income, recurring revenue, and building your business because I firmly believe this is the best way to achieve your financial goals without compromising your quality of life and personal fulfillment.

This book is intended to give you specific strategies to help you create wealth, freedom, and success in your life no matter where you are starting from today. Although the focus of the book is not on fulfillment, I hope to plant the seed that happiness comes from progress. It is the feeling that your outside world is aligned with your soul's purpose and that you are where you are meant to be and on the path that is unique to you.

I know as I sit here writing this that the vast majority of people do not feel that they are living a life reflective of who they really are or pursuing the things that really matter to them in a way that brings them joy and fulfillment. The reality is that we all have responsibilities, bills, and accountabilities to family and others, and sometimes we cannot just say, "I quit," or "I am leaving for Africa!" But that does not mean that you can't be taking action an hour a day every day until your dreams come true.

> "Nothing is impossible, the word itself says, 'I'm possible'!"
>
> ~Audrey Hepburn

I built my business while working full time. Not in a mindless 9:00-to-5:00 position but in a high-powered executive role for a Fortune 500 company. My responsibilities were crucial, the stakes were high, and I was held ruthlessly accountable for delivering results. So for the first few years of building my business, I worked before work and after work every day. You do what you have to do, no excuses.

No matter what your circumstances are, there is someone out there who would dream of being in your shoes. There are many excuses we can all make for why we are where we are rather than where we want to be, but the only honest thing you can do is commit to taking action every day until things change. People say, "Well I have so little time, it would be years and years before I can accomplish any reasonable progress." Think about that for a minute: The risk is that it takes longer versus it not happening at all!

So be aware that to create the next level of success in your business, career, life, relationships – whatever – it will be uncomfortable, you will have to do things you don't want to do or are even terrified of doing. Do it anyway.

If you are not willing to do something radically different, the results you achieve will be in proportion to that.

The final note I will leave you with before we dive into the first chapter is that no one else will believe in you and invest in you if you don't first demonstrate that you believe in yourself. You have to be willing to take risks, get out of your comfort zone, and demand what you want and deserve out of life if you are ever going to have a chance at actually achieving it. I hope this book inspires you to take a new action, accelerate the speed and aggressiveness with which you are moving toward your goals and helps you gain clarity on key strategies to help you get there.

Before you even get started on Chapter 1 of this book, I want you to *decide* and *take action* to *ensure* you achieve better, more profitable results.

Two things you can do right now that won't cost you dime but can literally change your life:

1. Go to iTunes or Sticher^{TM} radio and **subscribe to Unstoppable Success Radio.** This 30-minute, power packed show will give you the motivation, inspiration, and education you need to fuel your goals and achieve your dreams. There is a reason we have gotten more five-star reviews every day since its launch!

2. **Visit** www.kellyroachcoaching.com. When you arrive on the home page and scroll down, you will see the opportunity to **select from several different totally FREE trainings** to help you achieve your goals. Join my email community and put yourself in the company of thousands of other smart, driven, and successful entrepreneurs focused on growing their businesses and achieving their dreams.

PART 1:
FINANCIAL
ABUNDANCE

1

Stop Resenting the 1% and Join Them

Imagine yourself just hitting middle school – hyper aware and totally self-conscious...trying to balance school, friends, and hiding the fact that you are on the *free* lunch program. Growing up in a family of seven with a dad working at a nonprofit and a mom staying home to raise five kids, you can imagine there were many months where bills barely were paid, corners were cut, and there was constant stress about money. Yes, for many years we danced with the poverty line, but what we did have was an abundance of love which is what kids really need.

For me, I didn't care so much that we didn't have any money as much as I didn't want to stand out and be humiliated for it.

I will never forget the day there was a new lunch lady collecting our envelopes of money to pay for our meals. Mine of course was empty just like it was every day, only the other lunch ladies all knew we were on free lunches and never opened the envelope, instead just tossing it quickly in the pile. As she ripped open the empty envelope, I froze in complete horror so mortified that I still, to this day, don't even remember what I said or what happened next. My classmates who saw the fiasco were nice enough never to mention it, at least not to my face. What I knew for sure was that they didn't chalk it up to me just being my badass self, trying to pull one over on the lunch lady.

At that young age, I came face-to-face with total vulnerability and embarrassment because of our financial situation, a situation that I didn't sign up for, create, or choose to represent me... but it did anyway.

Although I didn't know it at the time, that experience triggered a decision that would quite literally shape the rest of my life. It was that experience that caused me to get very clear that I would not settle for what I was being handed, I would not have another person be the decision maker for me, and just because I was a kid and had to deal with those circumstances, in the future this would not be the case.

That decision in middle school has served me well. That's not the end of that story, but I will share more as we progress.

You probably noticed the title of this chapter: "Stop Resenting the 1% and Join Them." In reading that, perhaps you cringed. Perhaps you find yourself among those who do resent the 1%. Before you close this book and decide it's not for you because of this chapter's title, I urge you to keep reading. Your ability to achieve success is as much about mindset as anything else. Changing your mindset about this is the first step.

Having been someone who came from a situation where we were living just above the poverty line and now at the income level that hard work and determination has allowed me to achieve, I find the recent popularity around bashing the "1%" to be atrocious.

The last time I checked, America, with all of its flaws and imperfections, is still a country where – if you are willing to do the work, educate yourself, and not quit when the going gets tough –

anyone can become a millionaire. I understand that dependent upon where you are today this might sound ridiculous, but it's the truth.

The first step in bringing more financial abundance into your life is loving and respecting, not resenting, those who have done the work and, for the most part, earned their way to the top. Think about Bill Gates for a moment. He's one of the richest men in the world and clearly part of the 1%. Yes, a part of his success was "right place, right time"; however, you might be surprised to learn about his first company: Traf-O-Data. Never heard of it? That's not surprising. It failed miserably. Gates and partner, Paul Allen, created a device that could read traffic tapes and process the data. When trying to sell it, it didn't even work! Imagine that embarrassment. But they didn't wither away after that failure and any associated embarrassment. Allen actually attributed that failure to their future success, stating that it was seminal in preparing them to make the first Microsoft product a few years later.

> *90% of self-made millionaires achieved their wealth in their own businesses. According to Forbes, on the Forbes 400 billionaire list, 273 of them scrapped their way onto the list through their own efforts.*

Yes, it's a big world out there, and chances are you have encountered the good, the bad, and the ugly when it comes to money and wealth. My point is: Can you really aspire to and even attract something into your life that you resent? Seems a bit counter intuitive when you look at it like that, right?

Where are you sitting today? Maybe you already are in the "1%" or have made your first million and want to figure out how to get re-energized about what's next. Or maybe you are struggling – maybe it's been a rough run of job losses, business struggles, loads of debt. I get it. Maybe you are right in the middle – just comfortable enough that you are willing to stay miserable because to make a change seems like more pain (and effort!) than staying where you are.

> *There is a difference between wishing things were different working to make them different.*

No matter where you are, you are obviously reading this because you know there is more. You know that life has incredible abundance, joy, and happiness at a level that you have not yet tapped into, and you are probably wondering, "Is it really possible for me?"

The answer is yes! It is possible and available for everyone, but the truth is that a very small portion of the population ever challenges the status quo or attempts to change the things in their life that they despise or feel don't really represent who they truly are.

I am hoping we've crossed paths at a time in your life where you are hungry for something different. Now we all know that there is a difference between wishing things were different and living out what's necessary to make them be. Make sure that if you are not there yet, you work on getting your head wrapped around the mental aspect of this before you attempt the physical.

The exterior, physical changes that you want to see in your life take time, persistence, grit, and a whole lot of patience. If you are not mentally prepared to captain the ship, even the most skilled seaman will not cross the ocean successfully.

So let's start at the beginning. Your energy and thought process often direct how much money flows in and through your life. The first goal of this book is to impress upon you a few very important concepts as they relate to money so that you can benefit to the max from the rest of the book.

Money Mindset

Do you believe that a few years from now you can earn in a month what you previously did in a year?

I remember the first time I heard someone speak about money mindset and how this was possible. I thought to myself, "Yeah, I wish." Then I actually looked back and realized that it was that very year in which I earned more in one month than I did in my first year as a business professional when my entire annual salary was $36,000. If I did this once, could I do it again? You bet cha! But where does it all begin? Believing in your own self-worth.

When I thought deeply about how much income I wanted to earn annually and what I needed to charge hourly to achieve this, I found myself beginning to get a knot in my stomach thinking, "Do I really feel comfortable asking for that?" And there it was: my own self-sabotage standing in the way of getting what I wanted.

Have you ever had this experience? It's like you want to dream that big dream, you want to think it's possible, but then just as you begin to wrap your head around it, something says-"No, who do you think you are?"

Most of the disconnect between where we are and getting to where we want to be is all in our heads. One of the first things I do with new clients who join my programs is help them correct their mindsets around income and strategy around pricing. Whether it's your income as an employee or growth as an entrepreneur, you have to overcome this self-doubt to earn what you are truly worth.

The point of me sharing this story is while I consider myself a very confident, aggressive businessperson, I even found my own beliefs standing in the way of achieving my dreams.

I want to ask you now to complete the exercise below and see what feelings and beliefs come up for you:

What is your current projected income/salary for this year?

$_____

*How would your life change if you earned this amount **each and every month** a few years from now?*

_____

_____

_____

Do you believe this is possible for you?

_____

_____

Is the path that you are on right now able to make this a reality?

_____

_____

What thoughts or feelings just came up for you? Excitement, confidence, power? Or a sinking feeling that, yes, you would love for this to be possible but you simply don't see where or how you can make this happen?

The truth is most people don't even put themselves in the game.

If you want to double, triple, or quadruple your income, you have to get on a path and in a career in which this is possible.

If you are working a dead-end job with a potential for only a few-thousand-dollar-a-year raise, are you on a path that makes this possible? How many years of busting your ass and slaving away would it take to achieve this type of annual growth in your income? A few lifetimes, most likely. This is my exact point: You have to put yourself on the field and in the game if you want to achieve this type of exponential growth.

There are many ways that you can do this of course, my favorite being keeping 100 percent of the growth and profit earned in your own business. The bottom line here is that starting to build true wealth and financial abundance in your life begins with the mindset, thoughts, and beliefs that lead to actions, and only then can the real transformation begin.

5 Key Money Concepts

Here are my top five key money concepts to live by:

1. You are entitled to nothing but can have anything.

What bothers me most about the society we live in today is that somewhere along the way people became confused about who is responsible for what. You and only you are responsible for your personal affairs. Waiting and hoping that the government, a family member, spouse, or some other person or entity will swoop in and deliver the goods is a surefire way to guarantee misery and, in most instances, a disaster. On the flip side, I do believe that we all have within us the capability to make the choice to be extraordinary, to overcome the circumstances handed to us, and achieve whatever it is our hearts desire. When you take total accountability for where you are and place the responsibility squarely on your own shoulders to create change, you become extremely powerful.

Being empowered in your own life makes you realize that every day is a series of thousands of choices and that the small decisions are in fact the big ones and add up to create the sum of your life.

Are there areas of your life where you have been the victim versus the hero of your own story?

———————————————————————————

———————————————————————————

——————————————

What decisions can you start making right now and every day to take control of your situation to create the outcomes you really want?

---

2. If you want to create financial abundance in your life, there has to be a strategy, roadmap, and plan that you live by every day.

The most amazing part about what I do is that I get to help people make their dreams come true. People come to me when they are at a place of being clear on the outcomes that they want, but they are not quite sure how to achieve them.

My biggest piece of advice for anyone who wants to change their financial situation is to be *real* with themselves. The plan has to add up. If you are floating along the river of life hoping that somewhere along the way things will magically change, you will be bitterly disappointed. Creating exponential leaps in your income is done intentionally and strategically by having a roadmap, a plan, and a vehicle to get you there.

This means that 1+2 has to equal 3. The actions that you are taking daily combined with the path you are on have to put you in a position to achieve the financial abundance you want to accumulate.

The good news here is that you don't need all the answers and you certainly don't have to be good to get started, but as one of my mentors said, "You don't have to be good to get started, but you have to get started to get good." You will learn through experience, mistakes, and successes how to chart the course. There is also a multitude of experts, coaches, consultants, and mentors who are able to walk you through exactly how to do what you want to do. One word of advice: Make sure the person you pick has achieved what you want to achieve.

Are you on a path that when played forward over the next three to five years will allow you to achieve the kind of wealth you desire?

_____

_____

_____

Do you have a vehicle (business, career, etc.) that allows for this type of growth?

_____

_____

_____

What things do you need to start doing immediately to put yourself in the game?

_____

_____

_____

What resources, support, or guidance do you need to get there?

_____

_____

_____

3. However you plan on going about becoming wealthy, you must find a way to provide undeniable, quantifiable value.

To the business owner or entrepreneur:

> *"I can't change the direction of the wind, but I can adjust my sails to always reach my destination."*
>
> *~ Jimmy Dean*

Too many times, I see people try to start businesses because of a passion they have for something no one wants to buy. I also see many entrepreneurs and small business owners completely self-focused on creating products and programs that they think the market wants or needs but truly are not in line with demand.

Be smart. Chart your path forward wisely. Sell things that people want and do your research to align your sales and marketing in a way that speaks to their pain points and the areas in which they most want and need relief. As a business consultant and coach, many times I find the biggest thing holding people back from their income goals is themselves.

It is no secret that people buy based on a few specific wants and needs.

Why not position yourself to add undeniable value in an area that people are naturally most motivated to buy in?

_____

_____

Does your product, service, or business provide a quantifiable result?

_____

_____

Does your marketing clearly spell out how it solves an urgent and pressing need in an area in which people want solutions?

Here I want to add for small business owners and entrepreneurs that you must have a lifetime commitment to learning the craft of sales and marketing. Without this, it is very unlikely that your business will survive and thrive in the long term.

To the employee:

As much as I hear people complain about the economy, layoffs, downsizing, etc., I have never seen a situation in which the star performer in any organization was the one to be let go. (Yes, there are exceptions where full divisions or even entire companies shut down, mergers and acquisitions happen, etc.) I am not saying that good, hard-working people don't get some tough breaks – they do. What I am saying is that if you work for an employer and that is your path to creating wealth, you have to deliver value at such a high level that they will do anything to retain you AND that if they do need to make cuts, you are in the clear because they can't afford to lose you.

Get that? They can't afford to lose you. Somewhere along the way, people began to believe that everyone is entitled to a job, no matter what. The truth is that many employees have forgotten that their role in a company is to make that business more profitable, more successful, and more viable for long-term success. If you want to scale the corporate ladder and make your wealth as an employee, you'd better make sure you can answer unequivocally "yes" that you are creating all of the above for your employer, otherwise you are at risk.

If you are an employee, your number one job is to make yourself indispensable: make your employer money, solve pressing problems, and create and execute solutions in line with the vision and goals. This is how you create unlimited upward mobility in your job or career… and this is the key!

Does the organization that you work for have the ability to pay you what you are worth?

_____

_____

_____

Is there opportunity to move up six, seven, or eight times to grow your income significantly and is there a clear direct path and progression making this possible?

_____

_____

_____

Is your manager successful? Have they been able to achieve what you want to? If not, what makes you think they can get you there if they haven't been able to get themselves there?

_____

_____

_____

4. Your imagination sets the new bar and standard for where you can one day be.

To create a new level of wealth and income, you must first focus on stretching your mindset. Start making decisions from where you want to be, not necessarily where you are today.

This does not mean simply spending more. Many times when individuals hear something like this, they automatically think: buy the expensive car, buy the handbag, put expensive things on credit cards... because it feels and looks good. What you will find about people who build and sustain wealth is that they make decisions from the long view: Six months, five years, ten years from now, will I be glad I made this decision or wished I had done things differently?

Imagine how your life would change if you added an extra $10,000 or $100,000 to your monthly income. Allow your imagination to begin to create an emotional connection to what this would look like for you. Chances are it's not the actual dollars that would change your life but the life experience that would change.

What would you be able to do for your family if you were able to achieve this?

_____

Would you move?

_____

Pay off all of your debt?

_____

Buy a vacation property?

_____

Spend a month somewhere each year in total relaxation?

_____

Pay off your mortgage?

_____

Retire your spouse?

_____

All of these things are entirely possible for you, but you can't simply think the thought and then move on and expect anything to change. The thought has to lead to commitment and then commitment to action.

> *Your thoughts must lead to commitment and that commitment must lead to action.*

The action that will make these things possible is not solely about the proactive things you do to put yourself in a position to achieve them but also those things that you choose not to do to make these outcomes possible.

One of the most important lessons in business growth strategy is opportunity cost. With opportunity cost, for everything to which you say "yes" means you are saying "no" to something else. This means you have to choose your yesses wisely. The people who grow wildly successful businesses often say "no" more than they do "yes" because focus is power and allows you to build incredible momentum. These successful entrepreneurs focus on the opportunity cost.

Money works very much the same way as opportunity cost. For each money choice to which you say "yes," you are saying "no" to something else.

For example: If you choose to spend $40,000 on your wedding or a child's wedding, you are choosing not to pay off $40,000 on your mortgage or perhaps place a down payment on your child's home or your own vacation property.

> *"When your self-worth goes up, your net worth goes up with it."*
>
> ~ *Mark Victor Hansen*

You have to clearly define your value system as a person and then make your monetary decisions in alignment with them, so you are happy with the end result.

5. You are worthy.

You have to believe in your own self-worth before you can expect others to. This includes investing in growing your career or investing in your products or services as a business owner and entrepreneur.

No matter what challenges and setbacks you have faced on your journey, you have the power to create change and you deserve everything that your heart desires. Many times, it is hard to set high standards and fully live out what is necessary to achieve them because of the judgment you will face from others and the fear of failure. Do it anyway.

The only way you can break through your money ceiling is by proclaiming what you want and living every minute of every day in alignment with your goals. This is easier said than done, for sure. It is critical to surround yourself with other like-minded, success-oriented people who are also serious about changing their circumstances. This may mean joining a mastermind or coaching program if your circle does not include people who you aspire to emulate or who have achieved what you one day hope to.

I do a lot of coaching with business leaders in both corporate executive or CEO roles as well as business owners and entrepreneurs regarding pricing. I can tell you it is 99 percent a mental game. Your level of confidence in your pricing and the certainty that you present around why you are worth it largely determines your success in getting it. Pricing your business effectively is at the center of creating substantial income without working yourself into the ground.

A good health check on your confidence level in your pricing is a good way to check in on the health of your overall self-worth and how this will impact your income and financial situation.

Challenge yourself (and your team) to push the envelope in this area to try to increase the return you are getting for the work you are already doing in your business. The more confident you become in this area, the more you can empower your team to go after better quality business, higher paying clients, and more profitable endeavors overall.

Recap:

- ➤ If you are willing to do the work, educate yourself, and not quit when the going gets tough, you can become a millionaire.

- ➤ Resenting those who have achieved success does nothing but stand in the way of yours. Instead ask yourself, "How can I learn from or work with someone who has achieved what I hope to?"

- ➤ What is your money mindset? Do you believe you are worth it? Believe in your own self-worth.

- ➤ While money mindset is critical, you must also have a plan and roadmap to achieve success. It takes work, persistence, perseverance, and patience.

- ➤ Remember the five key money concepts:

- You are entitled to nothing but can have anything.

- If you want to create financial abundance in your life, there has to be a strategy, roadmap, and plan that you live by every day.

- However you plan on going about achieving wealth, you must find a way to provide undeniable, quantifiable value.

- Your imagination sets the new bar and standard for where you can one day be.

- You are worthy.

If you understand that most of success is your mindset, and if you are serious about growing your income and ready to remove all excuses and just want to get it done, visit __KellyRoachCoaching.com/guide__ and sign up for the free book guide that will take you from motivation to action. This book is not meant to just be read; it is meant to be acted upon. This free guide will help you do just that.

2

CULTIVATING AN ENTREPRENEURIAL SPIRIT

My other passion besides business is wellness and exercise-more specifically dancing! There is nothing that brings me more joy and happiness than blasting music and going crazy, dancing my heart out. I also have a total disdain for anything being done half-assed, and I hold myself to the highest standard possible in everything I do.

In middle school, I was recruited to become a competitive dancer at one of the best technical dance schools in the Tri-State area. I knew immediately that there was zero percent chance we could afford lessons at this school but that this was an incredible opportunity. After all, students from this school went on to become professional dancers, NFL cheerleaders, and performers on the most prestigious stages around the world.

My entrepreneurial spirit became alive for the first time somewhere around the sixth grade when I worked out a deal where I would clean the dance studio in exchange for classes. (My mom, the most selfless person in the world orchestrated the whole thing, of course and did this side by side with me for years.)

I'm talking scrubbing toilets and floors, emptying trash, and cleaning the mirrors to get them spotless... on my hands and knees, after school and on the weekends.

Joyce Crane, the owner of the studio, was an incredible mentor and one of the best and hardest coaches you could ever imagine. Until the last few years when dance shows became wildly popular, most people had no idea how hard the training is as a competitive dancer. Because I was late to the game, starting my technical training in middle school versus the typical starting age of two or three, I had to work three times as hard to keep up and progress through the classes with my age group. There were many days of holding back tears, either because my coach was screaming in my face or because I knew I was not where I needed to be to perform at the level I wanted.

Not only was this the first awakening of my entrepreneurial spirit that allowed me to believe that every NO can become a YES if you are willing to work for it, but it was also my first encounter with a brilliant coach.

As coaching is now my profession, I like to reflect back on the characteristics of coaches who shaped my life and allowed me to achieve success at a level I couldn't have otherwise. Many people think of getting coaching as a luxury. They think it is frivolous spending that you can engage in once you have already achieved success at a high level. The secret to all high performance is getting the right coach out of the gate. Athletically, in my career, and in my business having a coach who could take me to heights I didn't even know I was capable of achieving was critical. I would not be where I am today without the support, guidance and feedback of my coaches along the way.

This situation forced me to grow up and develop an extreme mental toughness... fast. Each day as the kids filed into the studio, they would see me there cleaning; it was embarrassing and exhausting, but I didn't care. It gave me an opportunity to gain access to some of the best training available practically free.

This is the first time I remember intentionally making the choice to risk being judged or ridiculed in order to better myself and create opportunities for my future. If my parents had simply footed the bill for me, I never would have developed the strength of character and the self-confidence to put myself in situations that had both the risk of failure but also the opportunity for greatness. This has occurred in too many situations to count in my life.

No one teaches you in school that to achieve greatness, you need to take risks. To go far, you need to put yourself out there in a way that makes you totally uncomfortable and, maybe most importantly, that it is all beyond worth it.

Too many times, we are cattle herded into living lives and making choices that are not in alignment with who we really are. Cultivating an entrepreneurial spirit in everything you do is a critical component to develop financial abundance and ultimately freedom.

What Is an Entrepreneurial Spirit?

- ✓ It is questioning everything and always asking yourself if there is a better way.
- ✓ It is knowing the reason why you do what you do and being extremely intentional about every component of your life.
- ✓ It is making bold, empowered decisions in your life that could potentially risk failure, time, embarrassment, and money because you know that status quo is not enough for you.
- ✓ It is not allowing someone else to "assign" what your time is worth but instead determining what your time is worth and acquiring the knowledge skills and expertise necessary to get it.

Perhaps the most important characteristic I emphasize every day to my clients is a willingness to take imperfect action. That is an entrepreneurial spirit. It is an unwillingness to let fear keep you in a box in your own life.

Imperfect action has defined many entrepreneurs throughout history. Thomas Edison may be history's greatest example of imperfect action. Of course, you know that he invented the incandescent light bulb that changed the world. It is sometimes called the most important invention since man-made fire. Coupled with electricity, it extended the ability to be productive after sunset, and that's merely scratching the surface of its impact. The most important thing to keep in mind about his invention is the number of failures. That number ranges anywhere from 1,000 to 10,000, and the exact number isn't the point. The point is that it's a big number. It represents a lot of imperfect action. Equally important is Edison's perspective about repeated failure (aka imperfect action): "I have not failed. I've just found 10,000 ways that won't work."

If you are concerned about failing (or being embarrassed by perceived failure), keep Edison's perspective and drive to continue taking imperfect action in mind. Decide your path and keep moving.

Cultivating an entrepreneurial spirit probably means you are putting a few key things in place in terms of how you create income:

1. You have multiple streams of income.

The way you get yourself into financial trouble is by going all in on anything. Times change… you can see whole industries being made and destroyed daily. It is absolutely reckless to put your whole financial future in someone else's hands (as an employee) or in one product, service or specialization (as a business owner). You will notice that most very successful entrepreneurs have multiple ventures going at any given time, many times in completely unrelated fields or industries. There is a reason for this. It mitigates risk. No one can predict when the next major shift culturally, economically, or in the global environment will directly impact your income sources no matter how great you are at what you do.

Now I do want to clarify the importance of **focus**. I am not recommending that you spread your energy all over the place on multiple ventures using so many different tactics and strategies that you kill your own success. What I am suggesting is that you avoid being tied to:

> *'Active Income'*
>
> *includes wages, tips, salaries, commissions and income from businesses in which there is material participation (Dictionary.com).*

- One source of clients
- One product
- One or just a few customers
- One form of advertising
- One source of all of your household's income

This is how you get yourself into trouble. Things change rapidly and sometimes without warning. I am sure you can recall countless stories of individuals in each of the situations above who wound up bankrupt, losing their house to foreclosure, blowing through their life savings because of a job loss, economy, business shift, etc.

How many streams of income do you have currently?

_____

_____

What is the next closest, most efficient business endeavor you can pursue in order to expand your income-earning potential and mitigate risk (within your current business)?

_____

_____

What skills, tools, resources or support do you need to get started?

_____

_____

What action can you take right away to get started?

_____

_____

2. You have active and passive income.

> **'Passive Income'**
>
> *Passive income is income received on a regular basis, with little effort required to maintain it (Dictionary.com).*

There is a difference between active and passive income, and you need both.

Active income means you need to get up, show up, and be involved in order to be paid. As a Business Growth Strategist, in order to be paid, I have to deliver coaching and consulting services to my clients. While on the flip side, the sale of my online training programs, this book in your hands or on your computer, and the audio programs I have created no longer require my involvement and over time will continue to play a bigger and bigger role in my overall income.

If you are an employee and lose your job or are unable to perform the duties of your position, your income vanishes. If you are a business owner and, God forbid, get in an accident or get sick, you are up a creek without a paddle.

Active income is where everyone gets started; however, in order to create lifelong financial security, you need to start generating passive income. You can earn this money even when you are not directly involved or even present. There are about a million different get rich quick schemes that promise income without effort, but it takes time and effort to truly begin generating reliable passive income. Does that mean it's not worth doing? Absolutely not!

If you added $100.00 a month of passive income to your household income each month for the next ten years, you would be generating $12,000 per month by the end of the ten-year period. Regardless of the time and effort required to create this, you can retire in comfort without having to worry about trading hours for dollars, slaving away at a job, or always being on the clock running your business.

Here are some common ways to start earning passive or residual income:

- Creating a product or service that does not directly require your involvement
- Royalties from books, license agreements or other forms of intellectual property
- Income properties and their rents
- Bank account interest
- Dividends and interest from investments like stocks and bonds (portfolio income)

What you will notice here is that the first two require a lot of work upfront, but then have significant lifelong earning potential that you can control. After those, you will find traditional ways to create passive income outside of your entrepreneurial efforts. While they are still considered "viable" options, for most people, at this time they have lost a lot of their power and earning potential due to changes in the economic environment and trends.

You may already be building some of these streams of income and, if so, good for you! If not, a great place to start is by participating in a direct-selling opportunity in which you can earn commission upfront but also make residual income on all of your customer's future sales and get a portion of the profit from their customers as well.

I suggest you begin here because it requires little to no upfront investment. Yes, it requires sales, and yes, it is work. No magic bullets here. However, if you are willing to put a little bit of energy into the pockets of your spare time, it could have a big payoff in the long term. Think: early retirement, financial freedom and more.

If you have a business already, take some time and think about how you can expand your business model to include offerings that do not directly require your involvement. For me, my infoproducts and membership sites allow me to make sales and deliver significant value without needing to be involved in delivering a service.

3. **You have recurring revenue in which you make the sale once and get paid over and over again.**

I cannot emphasize enough how important this is if you want to not only grow a wildly profitable business but do it in a way that allows you to maintain your quality of life. I constantly see business owners and entrepreneurs alike who wake up on the first day of the month and start from zero, trying first break even from last month and then attempt to exceed it. This rarely works.

It is critical to learn how to design and sell high-dollar packages that are delivered over a course of monthly installments (ideally 12) in which you sell one and get paid for repeatedly. This eliminates the peaks and valleys in your income and allows you to grow quickly and easily without needing hundreds or thousands of customers.

4. You have at least one business of your own doing six figures even if it's on the side.

Everyone needs at least one six-figure business even if it's on the side. I say this because too many times I see people fall victim to their circumstances that keep them stuck for years in mediocrity due to family obligations or similar circumstances.

Very specifically I want to emphasize that I know and understand that the days of people just up and quitting their jobs to follow their dreams are pretty much over. In fact, I did not have that luxury. I was and still am the breadwinner for my family. I worked from 5:00 to 7:00 a.m.

> "*Someone is sitting in the shade today because someone planted a tree a long time ago.*"
>
> ~ *Warren Buffett*

before work and from 6:00 until 10:00 p.m. after work for my first few years of my business while serving in an executive role for a Fortune 500 company. No one has it easy. Everyone has a thousand reasons why it's not viable or practical to start a business, make a change, or follow their dreams.

The flip side is staying exactly the same... play that forward ten years and there is your life. Whatever it is that is holding you back or preventing you from moving forward, you can trust wholeheartedly that there is someone out there right now with a tougher hand who is moving forward anyway. Take a chance, give it everything you've got, and believe in yourself enough to fight for your future.

If nothing else, use your lunch break. Take one hour a day to build your business, to change your life. Although it may seem like an hour a day can't change anything, this is dead wrong. In fact, I teach people specifically step by step how to do this in my program called The Freedom Shift.

5. You see problems and challenges as opportunities and move swiftly to capitalize on them.

Some of the greatest fortunes ever made were created during times of crisis. Some of the richest men in history created their fortunes during tough economic times, including the Great Depression.

I already mentioned Thomas Edison. He opened his laboratory in the middle of a recession. Bill Hewlett and Dave Packard began their partnership during the Great Depression, and *Fortune* magazine was launched in 1930, four months after the Wall Street crash of 1929.

With these examples in mind, there is simply no excuse to let perceived hardships stop you. Quite the opposite. Those with an entrepreneurial spirit will grab challenges and find solutions, knowing that the result can catapult them to extraordinary success.

An entrepreneurial spirit means you can see through the problems and challenges and identify that it is the crisis itself that creates the urgency and demand for a solution.

If you have never done so, do some research on supply and demand to gain a better understanding of how to capitalize on these situations.

This not only applies to entrepreneurs and business owners but to those who are building corporate careers. If you want to skyrocket your value and income – find the problem causing your firm the most pain, frustration, and profit loss and solve it!

Entrepreneurial spirit is not about talking the talk; it's about walking the walk. So many times you hear individuals complaining about their circumstances or even about things that they wish were different or that they would change. Talk is cheap. Rather that talking about it, focus on taking imperfect action over and over again until you hit your stride and start to see success.

6. You make short-term and long-term investments in different things that each plays a role in your accumulation of wealth.

Each type of income, investment, and venture you participate in plays a different role in how you will achieve your goals.

What makes sense in each situation depends on whether it is a long-term or short-term income source and how critical its role is in your overall income-earning potential.

Savvy business leaders ensure that they have a balance of both and that they have protection and padding regardless of swings in the market, economy, or business climate.

Fast Action Tip: Do you have a support system in your entrepreneurial ventures – people who are successful already doing what you want to do? Set yourself up for success by attending events, joining groups, and getting mentoring to help you along the way. Remember to seek and accept advice from those who are where you want to be, not those who are invested in you staying where you are.

Having an Entrepreneurial Spirit

More than anything, unleashing your entrepreneurial spirit allows you to live fully. When you overcome the fear of failure and begin to take calculated risks to create a better future for yourself and your family, your circumstances will begin to change. People and opportunities will present themselves to help you on your journey once you begin to open your mind to the possibilities available to you.

No, it's not always the easiest choice. Success is never a straight line. But you have to first put yourself in the game before you can score the big win!

Remember that there will be failures and setbacks along the way. Your entrepreneurial spirit guides you and reminds you that the future can be better than the present and you have everything necessary within you right now to create the change you want to see in your life.

How can you embody an entrepreneurial spirit in your current situation to start creating more opportunity for financial abundance in your life?

_____

_____

What actions have you not taken that would put you on the path to financial freedom?

_____

_____

Has fear of rejection, embarrassment, or failure prevented you from tapping into your true potential?

_____

_____

> *"Entrepreneurship is living a few years of your life like no one else will, so that you can live the rest of your life like no one else can."*
> ~ *Unknown*

Fear plays a huge role in the reason why people stay stuck for years, sometimes for a lifetime. I remember feeling embarrassed and wondering what everyone I knew was saying about me when I launched my business. I remember the fear of putting myself out there and risking failure in front of everyone. It is only when your desire for something better in your life becomes greater and more powerful than your fear that you can push through these emotions to take the actions that will create the results you want.

Getting super clear on your "why" will help you have a "home base" to return to each day that reminds you of the bigger reason you are doing what you are doing. Let yourself get attached to the outcome that you want but be flexible in how you get there. Know that every challenge, setback, and stumble is redirecting you to your ultimate destination.

Recap:

> ➤ Get totally clear on what you want to accomplish and then commit yourself to doing what's required to achieve it.

> ➤ You must risk being judged and overcome your fear of failure if you truly want to achieve success.

> ➤ With an entrepreneurial spirit, you question everything, are intentional about every component of your life, make bold and empowered decisions, and you alone determine your worth.

> ➤ Income aspects of the entrepreneurial spirit:

> - Multiple streams of income
> - Active and passive income
> - Recurring revenue
> - At least one six-figure business
> - See problems and challenges as opportunities and capitalize on them
> - Short-term and long-term investments

> ➤ Success is never a straight line.

> ➤ Get over your fear and get moving in accomplishing your dreams.

*Realize that you already have an entrepreneurial spirit? Ready to launch your six-figure side business? Just go to **KellyRoachCoaching.com/guide** and sign up for the free book guide to learn how you can design, launch, and grow your six-figure side business, even while working full time. I did it and you can too!*

CHAPTER

3

ACT LIKE A CEO IF YOU WANT TO EARN LIKE ONE

I auditioned for the Philadelphia Eagles Cheerleading Team at the end of my freshman year in college and became the youngest member on the squad.

Being an NFL cheerleader is a major responsibility for an 18 year old. This experience taught me to be disciplined, mature, and poised in a multitude of situations: from being on camera, to being regimented with my diet and sleep schedule, to being performance ready, to managing three jobs while carrying a full load of classes.

There is more to being in the NFL than showing up on game day. Many days I would leave mid-afternoon for practice and not get home until close to midnight. Game days were typically 14-hour days.

One of the things that everyone knows about most professional cheerleading teams is that every year they produce a calendar featuring its members. It's a big event, with a lot of promotion and media buzz, and everyone looks forward to it. Prior to my joining the team, the Eagles cheerleaders had always done a swimsuit calendar with photos shot off-site at an elegant, tropical island location. It was always the launching point for plenty of opportunities with other media coverage.

At age 18, I was excited just to be an Eagles cheerleader… I wanted to dance, perform and have some awesome experiences along the way. During my very first year on the team, they announced that they would no longer be doing a swimsuit calendar but instead would be doing a lingerie shoot. As a college freshman, there was no way I was doing a lingerie photo shoot. I could look ahead and see how this might damage future relationships and my reputation. It took a lot of courage for me to approach the organization's management and let them know that I wouldn't be participating.

I assure you, this was a pretty big deal. They weren't happy and did not look favorably on my decision not to participate. However, for me, it was about long-term thinking and decision making. Although it caused pain and frustration in the moment, to this day, I am very happy that I made the decision I did.

> *Make your decisions with your future in mind, even if that means some sacrifice today.*

With the title of this chapter – "Act Like a CEO If You Want to Earn Like One" – I mean: Make decisions and sacrifices in the short term with a long-term vision and plan in mind, operating three, four, five, or even six levels above where you are today. For me, I knew my career would be in the business world and that I would be a leader and public figure. At the time, I had no idea how that would actually look, what industry I might be in, or how it would all play out, but I did know that posing in lingerie was not the right decision for me. Now with a toddler daughter as I write this book, I am thankful beyond belief that I chose not to do that.

The consequence? I missed out on a big trip, a lot of publicity and media attention as well as many opportunities that came for all of the others on the team as a result of that photo shoot. It was a big decision point for me. But here's the funny part...and maybe you'll get a laugh out of it:

There was a huge reveal party planned with media and cameras and all of the executives from the organization. The whole event was being recorded with the cheerleaders unveiling the lingerie that they'd be wearing for the photo shoot. Although I wasn't part of the lingerie shoot, I was still invited to participate in the accompanying fashion show. So they sent me to a designer boutique for my outfit. And there it was: the ugliest, most repulsive brown suit that you could imagine. It was the least flattering thing I could possibly wear! I literally could not believe I was being asked to wear this... but I did and smiled and walked the runway with pride knowing that I had made the right decision for me, even if no one else agreed with it.

I'm sure they chose it with a wink and a laugh; it showed me (even at an early age) that making these decisions feels painful in the moment and that they are usually coupled with more negative than positive reinforcement.

Think back over your own experiences. You probably have a story similar to mine – something that you chose to do (or not do) that created difficulty at the time, but now you are grateful to have made the decision you did. Keep that in the forefront of your mind and recall it as needed when faced with similar tough decisions now and in the future.

On the flip side, maybe you made the wrong decision in the past in a particular circumstance, deciding in and for the moment rather than looking for the unintended consequences that would occur later. That probably caused you some pain and you're cringing about it now. I'm not asking you to dredge that up to open an old wound, but I do want you to remember it when faced with your future decisions as the impetus you need to decide with the future in mind.

In this day and age of increased desire for instant gratification – I want it now, now, now – it's really difficult for people to make decisions that will pay off in the future because there is usually no immediate gratification.

This is a huge driver of why people remain stuck in their financial situations, in dead-end careers, and in relationships that don't serve them. There's more immediate pain in making a decision that will pay off in the future than there is positive reinforcement in the moment. Because of that, people only dip their toe in the water and then run in the opposite direction.

Keys to Uncapping Your Earning Potential

I'd like to point out a couple key things to help you understand how your decision making is likely keeping you stuck right where you are.

If you want to earn like a CEO (think millions), you're going to have to act differently, be different, and have a much more long-range vision for your life and your career. If you're making decisions in the moment *for the moment*, chances are you might be happy and comfortable now, but three months, five years, or ten years from now, you'll look back and realize that your comfort in the moment is the exact thing that kept you stuck and miserable. You'll see it was the very thing that kept you from creating a breakthrough.

There are three keys to achieving what you really want: sacrifice, self-control, and perspective.

To help you understand this, I'll share another personal story. I had just started my first entry-level job and was making $36,000 a year in sales and recruiting for a Fortune 500 staffing firm. I choose this job because of the company's broad-reaching reputation with offices across the country and around the world. I knew that the opportunity was endless regarding how fast I could move up and how far I could go if I were willing to put in the work.

I wore a suit to the office day in and day out, without fail. My co-workers always asked me why. My answer? "As seriously as you take yourself is how seriously the people around you, and your leadership are going to take you."

For me, being in a suit every day when getting in front of customers and multi-million-dollar decision makers meant they would take me seriously and they did. The result was closing millions of dollars in sales in record time leading to my first promotion in a matter of months. The decision makers I was selling to didn't see a 22-year-old sitting across the desk; they saw a businesswoman who was there to make an impact and who could deliver the results they wanted.

Did I enjoy wearing a suit to work every day? No. Did I enjoy spending the little money I had getting them dry cleaned? No. Did I want to get up early every day to get ready and hit the office in full hair and makeup? No. But I was acting as the CEO of my life. I wasn't working for the $36,000 I was already going to get paid for the job I was in, I was working to get my next seven promotions, which I accomplished in a matter of eight years.

> *Age-old advice that underscores thinking and planning ahead: Don't dress for the position you have; dress for the position you want.*

Have you been making decisions about your career and your life from where you are today? Or from where you want to be?

If you want to be earning like a CEO, what changes do you need to make in the way you are running your business or the way you are managing your career?

_____

_____

What things are out of alignment with your vision?

_____

_____

Are you envisioning and positioning yourself where you are rather than where you want to be... whether it's three, four, five, or six layers above your current position?

_____

_____

Are you willing to sacrifice now to achieve much more success later?

_____

_____

For me, I knew that I was going to work 60 to 80 hours every week for my first few years in order to reach the goal I'd set for myself: senior leadership in the organization and a multi-six-figure income. This was my goal from day one, from the first step I took inside the door of the company. Every day was about doing what I needed to do to accelerate my path to my goal. Because I had the vision and was working every day toward a very clear and specific goal, I was able to make the *daily* decisions that were leading me in the right direction.

Are you clear about the path you need to follow to get from where you are to where you want to be?

_____

_____

Is there a solid road map?

_____

_____

_____

Are you looking down the road and making decisions now, regardless of the sacrifice they demand, that will serve you in the future, leading you toward your goal?

_____

_____

_____

Perhaps you don't quite know what the path should look like... or even how to envision your goal. If that is the case, now is the time for real reflection about it. You can't make progress toward uncapping your income potential if you can't envision it and can't see the road to reach it. If you think it is impossible – that your business or your career can't get you there – you'll have to make changes to get on the right path.

The Path to Greatness Has Tolls

Your path to greatness is all about mindset and imperfect action. You have to make up your mind that you are willing to forego immediate gratification to get where you want to be.

Doing what you don't feel like doing when you don't feel like doing it is the only way to achieve your dreams. Otherwise you are just wishing. Those who achieve greatness exert incredible discipline and employ long-range thinking and decision making even in the seemingly small things.

49

Growing your business is all about discipline, and discipline is all about doing what you don't want to do when you don't want to do it because you know it needs to get done in order to get from where you are to where you want to be. The vast majority of the population does not exert discipline in the right areas to even put themselves in position to have the potential to capitalize on the available opportunities. (Remember: the 1% is a small figure for a reason – most people aren't willing to do what it takes.)

Sacrifice is at the heart of what gets people to extraordinary levels of success.

While being an NFL cheerleader seemed glamorous to all my friends, it was not without a lot of work and a huge level of commitment and sacrifice. At that age, my friends were always out partying and having a good time on Saturday nights. On the other hand, I was in bed by 8:00 or 9:00 because I knew the next day would be a long, 14-hour one that demanded a lot of energy. I sacrificed the fun in the moment of Saturday nights to be at my best on game day.

Consider some of these "sacrifice to reach extraordinary success" examples:

You probably haven't heard of Do Won Chang but you are probably familiar with the popular clothing store, Forever 21. Do Won immigrated with his wife, Jin Sook, in 1981. He worked three jobs simultaneously (janitor, gas station attendant, and coffee shop help) while planning to open his first clothing store. Today, Forever 21 is a multi-national, nearly 500-store empire that generates about $3 billion in sales.

John Paul DeJoria, founder of John Paul Mitchell Systems, hawked his shampoo door-to-door while living out of his car. No stranger to hard times and hard work, he sold Christmas cards and newspapers to help support his family before he turned 10.

J.K. Rowling, author of the Harry Potter series, was living on welfare with a dependent child, and completed most of the first book in the series in cafes, sacrificing what most would consider a normal life. She's now estimated to be worth $1 billion.

It's those little decisions that lead to the big successes in life. People have a lot of misconceptions about how to achieve big successes in life. Everyone thinks that reaching success is a big transformation, a big happening, a big accomplishment that changed everything in a moment. In reality, when you study those who have achieved greatness in their lives and careers, whether financially, artistically, athletically or scientifically, you see that their success occurred through very small but disciplined and intentional actions that they took over and over and that they committed to with everything they had.

Understand that the big things are the little things and the little things will drive the big things in accomplishing your goals and dreams. You might want to re-read that sentence a few times. It's incredibly important and so often overlooked and misunderstood.

Creating a transformation in your business, career, and life – financially, successfully, or through complete fulfillment – comes down to you beginning to understand what the little things are that you need to do every single day that will create the massive change you are looking for.

Six- and seven-figure entrepreneurs will tell you that it is the small, disciplined actions that they take daily, the rituals they live by, and the commitments to which they adhere to, no matter what, that are the complete game changers in their lives. I can attest to this. There are rituals I live by and weekly commitments I make in my business that I make sure happen no matter what other sacrifice may be needed. These are the things that produce results for my clients and myself.

> *"Opportunity is missed by most people because it is dressed in overalls and looks like work."*
>
> ~ *Thomas Edison*

Sacrifice seems to have become a dirty word in our society. You only live once keeps appearing with greater frequency as the reason for doing things. While living in the moment is important, if you truly want to be part of the 1% and enjoy the benefits that come with that, you will have to sacrifice in certain seasons of your life. You are not giving up the rewards; instead, you are delaying them and will enjoy multiplied rewards in the future.

Self-Control

In many ways, your level of self-control impacts your level of success.

One of the easiest ways to think about self-control is to think about it from a nutritional and fitness perspective. Everyone is familiar with the impact and benefits of diet and exercise. Diet and exercise are really about self-control. Being healthy is about 80 percent nutrition and 20 percent of your overall well-being, and there is a balance. If you don't exercise self-control in the kitchen, you will have to kill yourself in the gym to maintain that balance. Conversely, using self-control in terms of your diet means your work out doesn't have to be so intense and you can still maintain a healthy physique.

> *Just as an individual's ability to delay gratification at a young age is a powerful predictor of future academic and professional achievement, discipline is also central to the long-run economic health of nations.*
>
> *~ Peter Blair Henry*

This is the most obvious analogy to the impact of self-control on your success. The less self-control you exert on the critical components of your business, the harder you're going to have to work in other areas of your business to make up the shortfall. Like diet and exercise, the key is balance.

The clearest business relationship regarding self-control that I see daily in my coaching business is clients failing to do enough profit-producing sales activities now and then having to work significantly harder down the road to achieve the same result. It is hard to watch because I can see how close those clients are to the tipping point of achieving what they want. If they would just have the self-control to do what's needed now, they would quickly reap all the benefits and rewards.

53

On the flip side, I can almost always tell within the first month when I have taken on a client who will be a rising star. They join one of my programs and within a matter of days are taking action on all the right things: sales, marketing, hiring, and building systems for success. The roadmap is available for everyone, but it is the individual who determines their own success or failure.

This is especially true in the realm of sales. Somewhere along the line, many entrepreneurs have developed a mindset that either selling is not required or isn't critical to building their businesses. The thinking is that you should be able to send out an email or push a button and your business will grow. If it doesn't, try the next hot Internet marketing strategy, spending more and more money trying to close a sale. I see entrepreneurs going out of business all the time, racking up hundreds of thousands of dollars in debt because they didn't invest in understanding the sales process and the marriage between sales and marketing – they work together to achieve success! This also occurs in the corporate environment.

Having marketing without sales or vice versa, you will continue to struggle. While there are exceptions (as there are to everything), the vast majority of businesses that go belly up do so because they are unable to close enough sales at a high enough level of profitability to be able to sustain and grow the business – covering both expenses and pocketing additional money for growth.

Whether you're an employee or executive trying to reach C-level status or you're a business owner or entrepreneur: Are you speaking with enough customers either face-to-face or at least voice-to-voice to close the level of sales you need to grow and achieve your income goals?

If you're a team leader (or a business owner with staff), have you invested what you need to in your team's coaching and training, including systems, processes, and accountability reporting, to ensure that you can close enough sales at the needed profitability each month to grow your business?

Do you have a handle on your database to which you are (or should be!) selling? Enough quality prospects that are being followed up on each week to drive the volume you need to achieve your income goals? Many business owners and CEO's totally lose sight of this as one of their most critical responsibilities. What could be more important than the list of companies or individuals that all of your future sales will come from. It's not just what's in the database that's important, but the quantity and quality of the activity and how the whole process and system is being managed.

> *"It is in your moments of decision that your destiny is shaped."*
>
> *~ Tony Robbins*

With most entrepreneurs and small business owners, it almost always comes down to one of two things: undercharging or sales. They simply don't have enough profitable sales closing each week to achieve their goals.

Many business owners struggle because they have employees who are not covering their own incomes. It's not the employees' responsibility to figure out what they're supposed to do to cover their income and produce a profit. It is your role as the business owner or leader to provide structure, processes, systems and accountability to ensure their daily actions and tasks are going to put them in the position to produce income and profit for your business.

You must have self-control to overcome your fear and discomfort of what you need to do, so you do it anyway. If you're serious about creating a transformation in your life and business, you must gain control of self. You can't control anything around you if you can't first control yourself.

It means you have to check your ego and be willing to admit the role you play and the areas in which you've fallen short. You must take total ownership and accountability for being exactly where you are and own the changes you will need to make in order to change your outcome. You have to find the internal locus of self-control. There's no pointing the finger at your staff, your colleagues, your boss, partner, investor, the economy, or your competition. Your achievement failure is not the fault of any one of those things. You own it and are fully responsible for all of your outcomes. When you hand over control by blaming anything or anyone else, you give up the ability to design your own destiny.

The other key to self-control is learning to take nothing personally. This is another area in which I find people struggle immensely when it comes to growing their businesses or advancing their careers.

In order to accelerate, you have to be willing to have someone look you in the eye and tell you clearly and directly – *without you taking offense* – what you have to do differently. You need to be able to hear it, and the speed with which you can hear it and heed it is the speed with which you can change your outcomes and income. Many don't even solicit feedback because they don't want to hear the answer. Or if they do, they don't really listen and apply what they've heard.

I have been talking about the importance of having a coach or mentor. You truly do need someone outside of yourself, looking at everything you're doing and pointing out what you're are missing or failing to see. Trying to go at it alone improves the odds that you will miss critical decisions and actions along the way (and risk being one of the 80 percent of businesses that fail, I might add).

For me, what has been so powerful about working with a coach is the ability to learn the exact strategies and systems they utilized to get to where they are (which is where I wanted to be). However, hiring a coach in no way guarantees results or success. Hiring the *right* coach and matching that with action, commitment, passion and follow through… now that pretty much guarantees success.

Taking nothing personally empowers you to shorten the time it takes to *exponentially* increase your income. Do not fear rejection. If you don't put yourself out there and allow for rejection, you are also then failing to put yourself out there to allow for success! Welcome criticism and judgment. Without looking for it, you are also not being heard by those who want and need your products and services. You have to expose yourself to negative feedback and attention in order to get positive feedback and attention. Otherwise, you are keeping yourself hidden.

You must remove emotion and think strategically. Your decisions must be based on strategy. It's an easy trap to fall into. We're emotional by nature. When you need respond to a critical situation or make an important decision, do not do so immediately. Take the time needed and think it through to better ensure the correct decision. On the other hand, there is a reasonable timeframe for decisions and then there is paralysis by analysis. If the decision is so unclear to you, either seek guidance (from the right sources) or ask a different question.

> *"Leave your ego at the door every morning, and just do some truly great work. Few things will make you feel better than a job brilliantly done."*
>
> ~ Robin S. Sharma

Respond from your higher self that has the vision of the future rather than from your lower self – your ego – that wants immediate response. Time and space (how and when you respond) is the difference maker in the ability to make the right decision and take the action that will garner the results you want.

Perspective

In order to have perspective, you must have a long-range vision. It's all about your ability to see the bigger picture and to make decisions that keep you on track for your long-term goals and dreams versus just satisfying a momentary want or need.

Many times when I ask individuals about their long-range vision and goals, they often don't truly have a sense of where they're going and what they want to achieve. They're trying to make it from one day to the next and only focus on achieving an immediate short-term objective. While specific focus on short-term goals is important, you will end up only making decisions based on short-term thinking. This decision-making strategy will fail to serve you in making proactive leaps in your income. You may make it over the finish line for that week or month, but you will not be making the decisions that will set you up to increase your income into the multi-six- or seven-figure range.

Before continuing in the book, I want you to design or revisit your long-term vision for your business, career, and life.

Define where you want to get to in the next three to five years.

_____

What does it look like?

_____

What components does it have?

_____

I had mapped out my income streams and silos of my business before I even got my first client. Did things change and my goals adjust? Absolutely! However, my long-range vision allowed me to achieve things in my first few years that for many business owners it may take five to ten years to accomplish. I worked backward from where I wanted to be in my decision making. Subsequently, these steps created big leaps in my business rather than just getting the next paying client.

You can't make an impactful, results-generating decision if you don't understand what it is you are really trying to achieve.

A lot of people admit are simply trying to get through the month or get out of debt. Perhaps you are in that position and that's why you are reading this book. Keep in mind that if you set the bar at "getting out of debt," you will very likely get there. But don't you want more? When you get out of debt, then what?

Set your vision and mindset well beyond that! Achieving a low bar and goal will not create an extraordinary shift in your income or transform your life. I want you to achieve more… to be able to do things for yourself and your family that you haven't been able to do or that you perhaps thought were impossible to achieve.

Having a personal mission statement and value system that you live by and that represents you is a great way to ensure your decisions are in check and you are satisfied with your outcomes. It will also allow you to make decisions fast.

Successful people are decisive and make decisions quickly. Once they do, they own it and go forward with it and course correct as needed.

Take a few moments and write out your value system.

- *What is important to you?*
- *What values do you want to represent you?*
- *How do you want people to describe you?*

_____

_____

_____

_____

_____

_____

Next, spell out how you describe your personal brand – your energy, look and feel.

What words would someone use to paint a picture of who you are? Or write how you would want someone who does business with you to describe the experience.

_____

_____

_____

_____

_____

_____

Take the time to do this because when you understand your vision and have absolute clarity about what you want, money will be attracted to you.

Money likes speed. When you're clear on your decision-making tree – your values, your vision, and personal brand – it's much easier to make a fast decision.

Answer these questions:

Is this in line with who I am?

In line with the person I want my children to see?

In line with the kind of business I want representing me?

When you can answer these questions in a split second, decision making becomes easy and you can stay in action, which is critical to success.

Be That Person Now

I want you to keep thinking about whether or not you are allowing yourself to live fully in alignment with who you are as a person now. Or are you saying, "I'll do that when..."

Many people delay launching a business, waiting for the right time. The truth is there is never a good time... or the right time! Not one of my clients (and they run the gamut!) would say it was good timing to launch their businesses or take that huge career step.

Are you living in alignment with who you really are right now? Or are you putting off making the decisions that will shatter that glass ceiling over your income potential? Every minute that you delay or say you'll "do that when...," you are minimizing the chances of doing it *ever*!

Start following your dreams and making the right decisions now. Take one hour every day. I understand all of the things that may be impacting your life right now – family, kids, aging parents, debt, work requirements, household needs, responsibilities… I get it. This is why I encourage you to find people who inspire you and have accomplished what you one day hope to and study their story. You will find that they struggled through situations and obstacles just like what you are facing but they pushed forward in spite of them.

At times, you may feel like you don't have one more ounce to give. I want you to dig deep and remember the life you are trying to create. Just keep putting one foot in front of the other, you can do this!

> *It's about living your life now like no one else will, so you can live your life later like no one else can.*

Start by applying the 80/20 rule and eliminating those things in your life that don't or no longer serve you: the things you've done because you've always done them or things you do out of guilt. When you cut these out of your life, you open hours of time that you can redirect to building what you truly want.

It is sacrificing in the short term, but you will end up being a happier person… because happiness comes from progress. Progress is about taking daily actions in alignment with who you really are and moving toward your goal… being in alignment with your soul's purpose and achieving what you were put on this planet to do!

Be open and evaluate where you can cut things out of your life to be able to move toward your goal. Perhaps it's discipline – saying "no" to things or people that no longer fit with your true vision and goals for your life. Perhaps it is creating healthy boundaries in your existing career or business to make space for something new. Or maybe even it's time to cut out television and other habits that keep you where you are versus making your goals a reality.

To reach your goal, you have act like the CEO of your life *now* if you want to earn like one later.

Recap:

➤ As difficult as it may seem now, make your decisions with an eye on the future and keep in mind that the choice you make today must align with your vision for your future.

➤ Act, think and make decisions in alignment with where you want to be. Remember: Don't make decisions for the position you have today; think, act and decide for the position you want tomorrow.

➤ You must gain complete clarity about where you want to *be* before you can envision the path that will take you there.

➤ Success doesn't occur in one grand moment; it results from the daily decisions you make, and yes, there will be sacrifices along the way.

➤ Success and self-control are directly proportionate. Do what needs to be done now, or you will be working far harder in the future to achieve the same thing.

➤ Sales and marketing are two sides of the same coin. You need them both!

➤ Remember your perspective. Don't focus on today; focus on your end game.

➤ Envision who you want to be and start being that person now.

It's very simple but sound advice: Act like a CEO if you want to earn like one. Need to raise your prices and get serious about being the CEO of your company vs. your company's Super Employee? Get started making the shifts necessary to achieve your ultimate goals today. Go to: KellyRoachCoaching.com/guide and sign up for the free book guide.

PART 2:
FREEDOM

CHAPTER

4

LEADERSHIP

The sad but honest truth is that freedom is not so free. It is not true for the freedom of the nation, and it is not true for the freedom in your own life.

There is a price you pay for freedom and a lot of it comes down to what we covered in the last chapter: sacrifice, self-control, discipline, and perspective.

In a world where it has become continually more demanding to keep up with the costs of everyday living, family obligations, and simply handling everyday trials and tribulations, how do you create freedom?

For me, the price was a whole lot less freedom before I gained more freedom in every stage of my life. In my corporate career, I was always the one working nights and weekends during my first few years… certainly less freedom for me. But the result was that within a few years, I was in at 8:00 and out by 5:00 while still generating some of the best results in the company.

When I started my business, I was not in a position to leave my role as an executive, so it meant once again returning to working nights and weekends. Once again, less freedom. However, within a few years, I was earning more in my business part-time than most entrepreneurs ever do working full time.

Beginning to see a theme here? I share this not to impress you, but to impress *upon you* that freedom has a price... and unless you are willing to pay it, there is no way in hell you will get and keep freedom in your life.

Perhaps the most important element of creating freedom in your life is your ability to impact and influence others to get results on your behalf: a little thing I like to call leadership.

There is no one I can think of in history who achieved extraordinary things alone. Just because they were the "face" of change, leadership, a business, etc. did not mean there was not a village behind them making it all possible.

> *The best description of leadership I ever found: "If your actions inspire others to dream more, learn more, do more and become more, you are a leader."*
>
> ~ John Quincy Adams

I read this quote from John Quincy Adams daily and try to live this in my interactions with others every day. This does not just apply to a job title or role as an employer; this is the essence of how you can create exponential impact and influence in every interaction you have with another human being.

I see leadership evolving through three stages with each stage creating greater freedom in your life:

- Impact
- Influence
- Legacy

If there is one personal characteristic to develop to create more freedom in your life, it is leadership. It is leadership that eliminates all boundaries on what you can accomplish, and it creates an endless sea of opportunity for your future.

Impact

Let's start with step one, impact. Your first step is to become an expert at whatever it is that you do and the necessary complementary skills needed to create income and freedom with it.

Impact will primarily serve as a foundation for influence and legacy. You cannot empower knowledge, understanding, or expertise that you do not yourself possess. Your ability to teach others a replicable and valuable skill will be critical in creating time, location, and financial freedom.

In my own career, my first step was becoming a master sales closer. I first perfected my ability to close six- and seven-figure clients and to do it rapidly, consistently, and predictably. I studied sales books and practiced. I took every piece of feedback my manager and coach gave me and implemented it immediately to try to get better as fast as I possibly could. The primary skill was the ability to close clients effectively, but I also needed to be able to navigate pricing negotiations and get the right decision makers to sign off on the deals.

I knew that I wanted to move up in the company very rapidly, and the way to be noticed by upper management quickly was through closing a ton of sales fast and making sure that they were profitable and ideal clients for the firm. I chose to become good at the skill that was considered most valuable in order to advance.

What skill do you need to develop as a business owner, entrepreneur, or leader right now that will open up your ability to grow your career and income quicker?

_____

_____

_____

_____

_____

Who can you model, learn from, or associate with that is exemplary in this area?

_____

_____

_____

_____

_____

> *"The quality of a leader is reflected in the standards they set for themselves."*
>
> ~ Ray Kroc

Picking the right area in which to make an impact is as important as the ability to make the impact itself. Too many times I see people working very hard at perfecting all the wrong things... things that are not going to improve or change their situations. Be strategic and choose wisely on where to focus your energy. Look down the road and ask yourself if this area of impact is going to create lasting change in your life.

The best business coach I ever had was my boss, Dave. He beat into my head that no matter how much of a sales superstar I became, there would always be a limit to how much even the world's top sales person could produce. Of course this makes sense, but once again that word "sacrifice" creeps in. I would have to sacrifice my own personal performance and risk potentially putting in more hours (less freedom) to help make others successful.

One complaint or hesitation that I hear from my clients a lot is that they hate investing in hiring, coaching, and developing a team because many times, employees don't work out or you train them and then they end up leaving. This attitude perpetuates you to forever being a producer... essentially a hamster on a wheel. Unless you are willing to forego that attitude, you will always hit a ceiling, like my Boss Dave instilled in me: There would always be a limit to how much I could do on my own. Yes, there are always challenges when you are working with people, but there are many things you can do to mitigate the risk and improve your chances of success. I encourage you to do your own research in this area as the topic exceeds the parameters of this book.

The bottom line in making employees successful and getting out of the producer role and becoming the CEO of your career or company is that more than 80 percent of your employees' success or failure depends on you. If you want to create freedom in your life, you have to commit to becoming a strong teacher, coach, trainer, and manager; it's par for the course. Their success depends on you, and your ability to grow depends on them.

Your ability to create freedom in your life and business depends on your ability to inspire, empower and engage contractors, employees, vendors, partners and investors to help you achieve your goals. First, you must demonstrate authority, expertise, and impact to get others behind you with their support to make your dreams a reality.

In many ways, your ability to excerpt long-range thinking and decision making to create options determines your freedom. You need to have many choices to create freedom. This means you are always looking at the big picture and thinking strategically so that you aren't backed into a corner and end up making poor decisions that steal your freedom.

To me, freedom means being in control of my own outcomes, deciding what my time is worth, and deciding my own destiny. That is why I truly believe that if you want more freedom in your life, it is essential to have at least one business of your own.

What does Freedom mean to you?

_____

_____

What changes do you need to commit to making now in order to achieve true and lasting freedom in your life?

_____

_____

Influence

This brings us to step two in the process of creating freedom in your life: influence. I like to think of influence as the ability to get results through others. Once you have identified the core skill set you need to create unlimited success and have perfected your ability to deliver results, it's time to begin to enroll others in your vision.

> *Management, training, coaching, and leadership are necessary for success, but they are not the same.*

Most people move from being a producer to a manager but never master leadership which is why they fail miserably, turn over their staff, and end up burnt out and exhausted – right where they started. They're no closer to their goal, only tired.

I always tell my coaching clients that it is important to understand the distinction between management, training, coaching, and leadership. Each of these unique competencies and focus areas plays a critical role in how well a company, team, or division succeeds. It is possible to succeed without one of these, but your results will be immeasurably better when leveraged together properly.

Not enough emphasis is placed on teaching people how to authentically influence others in a way in which everyone wins, so there's a simultaneous promotion of all interests. This is the art that true leaders have and use to achieve extraordinary results and gain loyalty, commitment, and passion from others to assist in achieving their missions.

So how does the ability to influence others create freedom in your life?

Truth be told, it is really the *only* way to create freedom. Most business owners do not operate as the CEOs and visionaries of their companies. They are self-employed in a job in which they get paid less and work more than they did in the past. Why? Because they lack leadership; they are the super employee in their business rather than the president of their company.

The same goes for most managers in larger organizations. Most leaders work harder and longer hours than the employees who report to them. Why? Because they lack leadership. Instead of coaching and developing others to stand on their own two feet and to be empowered to take ownership in their roles, they either manage them without coaching, systems, and accountability producing only short-term results or keep their hands in everything to such an extent that the business can't function without them.

Have you fallen into either of these traps?

_____

_____

Now is a good time to assess your leadership strengths and weaknesses to determine what changes you need to make to start creating freedom in your life. The following questions are great indicators to determine if you are still acting as a producer or have begun to demonstrate true leadership.

Take some time now to take this leadership assessment and see how confident you are in the path you are on:

Leadership Assessment

Do you spend a significant amount of time investing in growing and developing leadership among those on your team?

_____

_____

Do you separate out the genius work that you should be doing from the tactical tasks that should be outsourced, delegated, or eliminated all together?

_____

_____

Are you able to attract and retain top performers? What is your turnover rate?

_____

_____

Do you work to make your team, division, or company an employer of choice for which the top available talent wants to work?

_____

_____

Do you value and integrate the feedback from those who support you to take your business or career to the next level?

_____

_____

How much of your time is spent doing versus thinking and strategizing?

_____

_____

Do you have detailed training and coaching processes to make those who work for you successful?

_____

_____

Do you test and measure what works and what does not and challenge the status quo in an effort to achieve superior performance and results?

_____

_____

_____

Are you able to take complex problems and break them down into simple, powerful strategies that can be executed by a team?

_____

_____

_____

Do you achieve exponentially better and more results now through a team than you did at your peak as an individual performer?

_____

_____

_____

Have you designed and begun teaching replicable processes for achieving results in your field that you can quickly and easily teach to others?

_____

_____

_____

Are you focused on either short-term production goals or long-range scale, or rather an ideal balance of the two?

_____

_____

_____

Is your number one focus your personal results, or do you focus on how many others you can make successful?

_____

_____

_____

Do you inspire those who come in contact with you to perform at a level beyond what they thought they were capable of?

_____

_____

_____

Are you focused not only on making an impact but on making a difference?

_____

_____

Do those who you want to follow you trust you, respect you, and willingly follow your guidance?

_____

_____

Are you comfortable willingly owning your imperfections, mistakes, and learnings rather than hiding them or placing blame outside of yourself?

_____

_____

When you step into true leadership, your focus shifts from a focus on self to a focus on others. To become an extraordinary leader is to genuinely love making others successful.

The best way I can describe the relationship between the leader and the team is that the leader should work as hard, if not harder, at making the team successful as they expect their team to work to achieve the expected goals and results.

In order for leadership to begin to create freedom in this stage, you need to put the following in place:

- Systems
- Processes
- Accountability
- Checks and balances

Mobile accessibility to all of the above is critical in order for you to keep the pulse of what is happening and maintain control without being physically tied to any specific time boundaries or locations.

The easiest way to uncap your income and create a totally safe, guaranteed-for-life career for yourself is by making others successful. Something to think about when you are choosing your profession or the next business in which you get involved.

Legacy

The third and final step in your leadership evolution occurs when you begin to focus on legacy. Legacy is what you leave behind: the difference you make, the lives you touch, the reach your mission and work has in the world beyond your lifetime.

You can begin to focus on this aspect of leadership at any time you choose, and it's when you begin to operate above and beyond ego. It's when you begin to make decisions and take action from the bigger picture of your life and the meaning you want it to have had in the world. When you focus on building legacy, you are no longer in the box of income or ego – you are now fully in your higher self and what you want your life's work and message to be beyond your years.

Perhaps you're thinking that with all of the day-to-day demands you have between your business (or your career), your family (kids, spouse, aging parents with their own needs), activities, kids' activities, exercise, hobbies (if you even allow time for those) and oh yeah, sleep, there is no time to begin thinking about your legacy. Many don't begin to think about legacy until toward the end of their life at which point for many it is too late. They don't think about it because they are too wrapped up in the daily demands that I've listed. It's very much like delaying retirement savings until later because there are more pressing issues now on which to spend money.

> *If you focus on making enough other people successful, you will always be successful.*

I'm certain you understand that you can't start retirement savings when retirement looms just ahead of you. Legacy is much the same way. You can't build it at the end of your life. You must start building your legacy today (if you haven't already started) in the same way you must begin saving for retirement long before you reach that milestone.

If you believe that your legacy will take care of itself, I want you to understand that it's far better for you to control it, and you can take control of it by determining what it is you want it to be and taking action toward it. A great way to create freedom and financial abundance at an accelerated rate is to begin thinking about legacy now.

If you start thinking about the legacy you will leave behind, you will quickly realize that you need many ambassadors for your mission, and in order to achieve this, you need to be a genuinely impactful and inspiring leader.

What legacy do you want to leave behind?

_____

_____

_____

_____

How many generations of your family do you want to impact? How do you want to impact them?

_____

_____

_____

_____

What do your actions, thoughts, and behaviors need to reflect now in order to achieve this?

_____

_____

_____

_____

You now know the three stages of your leadership evolution and how they impact your ability to achieve freedom. Clarity is power, so start by determining what type of freedom is most important to you: time, location, financial, etc. and begin to align your plan for how to leverage leadership to achieve your goals.

Recap:

➢ As with other elements of success, freedom comes with a price. You must first sacrifice in order to attain the freedom you want.

➢ Your ability to create freedom is directly proportionate to your ability to impact and influence others – the essence of leadership.

➢ In order to make an impact, you must first master the skill set that sets you apart, but ensure you are perfecting that which will make a difference.

➢ There is a limit, no matter how good you are, to that which you can produce. In order to break through that, you must employ and lead others.

➢ You must learn to influence others or you will remain as an employee in your own business rather than the CEO.

➢ The true leader relishes in making others successful, creating promotion for all.

➢ Nearing the end of your life is not the time to consider your legacy. Consider your legacy now and make every decision with it in mind in order to continue building it.

Leadership is essential to business growth. To learn more about mastery of all of the core competencies required to build and grow a million-dollar business and beyond, visit KellyRoachCoaching.com/guide and sign up for the free book guide.

5

BUSINESS MASTERY

During college, I had at least three jobs at any given time, ranging from aerobics instructor to nanny to NFL cheerleader... and I was even a cocktail waitress in one of the local bars. I share often with my clients and subscribers that the very things that you think have held you back in life are the greatest blessings you will ever receive. For me, growing up with financial struggle was the best thing that ever happened to me. Most people hold on to their wounds like trophies and let them seal their fate rather than strengthening their character. I want to challenge you to look at whatever you have struggled with or are currently challenged with through this lens: Determine how it is a blessing to you.

Everyone has a story... and I mean everyone. I am a firm believer that the human experience comes with chaos, challenges, and storms to be weathered. Your response and ability to take what is handed to you and turn it into gold comes down to your attitude, perspective, and ultimately the skill set that you acquire, refine, and use each day to deal with "life."

Of the many jobs that I held during my college years, cocktail waitressing taught me the most about business. It took me only a few nights on the job to realize that "good things come to those who hustle." I would leave at the end of the shift with literal wads of cash, sometimes in excess of $300.00 a night, not bad for a college kid serving drinks in a bar!

So why am I talking about cocktail waitressing in a chapter about Business Mastery and Freedom? There is a huge lesson here that I have applied to everything I've done in my life ever since and am convinced it has been the catalyst for building millions in business and helping others do the same.

You can show up, clock in, and take what's handed to you, or you can go in and set things on fire, squeezing every ounce of juice out of every opportunity you see. Two people can have the exact same circumstances, intelligence level, and amount of talent, but the person who sees the opportunity and seizes it with vigor will always come out on top.

When I realized that the little bit of extra hustle amounted to huge dividends in a very short period of time, I took that principle and applied it to my career. It got me promotions, but more importantly, it helped me help others rapidly advance their own careers. I could literally take a person who had never sold a day in their life and turn them into a selling machine in a matter of a few months. My teams broke every record in the company for growth, profit, pricing, internal promotions, expansion and more.

This is how I earned the reputation of a "Rapid Results Coach" and a "Time Compression Expert." I teach people how to do something in a matter of months that would otherwise take years. This can be applied to sales, growing your business, accelerating your career, and so on. Once you understand the levers that you have to pull to get results, it is very easy to gain control and direct your outcomes.

When I realized that I had a gift for business growth strategy, I knew I needed to share it. I also selfishly knew that if I could produce millions in profit for a corporation, I could also do the same for myself. Starting my own business was literally the only way to achieve my income *and* lifestyle goals. I stress the "and" because most people think you have to sacrifice one to get the other. I used to be one of those people until I discovered entrepreneurship.

Achieving More Through Entrepreneurship

I started Kelly Roach Coaching to help people achieve freedom, fulfillment, and financial abundance in their lives, businesses, and careers. My mission is to empower as many people around the world as possible with the skill sets, tools, resources, and strategies to take complete control of these three areas. I want you to do the same and live a life on your own terms.

What I did not understand or anticipate going into this business was how little the average person in business actually understands about how to go about achieving these things. The majority of my clients are business owners, entrepreneurs, and executive leaders. When they come to me, they are clear on a few things:

1. They are not satisfied with where they are.

2. They need help to create the changes they want.

3. They will not tolerate staying where they are for one more day.

I cannot stress enough that if freedom, fulfillment, and financial abundance are important to you, you need to make business mastery an ongoing commitment in your life.

The chance of finding a *job* that fulfills all three of these areas for you is slim to none. In fact, I have never seen it. Most people go through life knowing that they are capable of more and wanting more but never really taking drastic and lasting action to do something about it.

In today's economic climate, it is quite risky – if you are a primary breadwinner for your family – to rely solely on an employer for your income. This means that someone can literally wake up on the wrong side of the bed one morning and make a decision that has a devastating impact on you, your career, your financial stability, and the welfare of your family. Your whole future is in their hands… not the place you want to be.

I feel strongly that each family should have at least one six-figure business, even if it's on the side. In fact, I am so committed to this concept that I created a program specifically for executives who want to launch their own businesses while working full time.

I want to emphasize again that I built my business while working as a senior executive. I was managed very closely and held ruthlessly accountable for results. I was also responsible for coaching, developing, and managing 50 other individuals while in this role. I understand that everyone has obligations and responsibilities and most people today can't simply throw caution to the wind and "follow their dreams," but this is no excuse not to protect your future.

As a CEO of my own company, I spend hours every week developing and strengthening my own business knowledge and acumen, so I can continue to create a leading-edge company and deliver top-of-the-line results and strategies for my clients.

Now it's your turn. Is it time to reinvigorate your commitment to growing your business? Is it time to take a business that feels like more like a job than a source of freedom and make the changes necessary to transform it?

If you have not yet begun your entrepreneurial journey, how about beginning the process by dedicating just an hour a day to building passive income or getting your side business going?

And finally…whether you are a business owner, entrepreneur or employee, it's time to ask yourself if you have made the commitment to mastering the skills and competencies truly necessary to achieve your goals and get started today on creating that next level of success.

Don't Become a Statistic

It blows my mind how many people are in business today yet have no understanding of the basic principles needed to be *successful* in business. You can't become a millionaire, live and travel around the world on your terms, and enjoy doing work that you love without a plan…

> *"We have forty million reasons for failure, but not a single excuse."*
>
> *~ Rudyard Kipling*

Here is a snapshot of what is happening out there right now with most businesses:

- More than 80% of businesses fail in the first three years, according to Forbes.
- More than half of small business report **revenue at under $50,000**, according to a BusinessKnowHow.com survey.
- The number one reason for entrepreneur burnout and business failure is running out of money, according to David Goldin, CEO/President of AmeriMerchant. Running out of money is primarily driven by a lack of profitable sales!

I cannot think of a time when I met an entrepreneur who thought they were signing up to work more, earn less, and burn themselves out for enough income to barely get by when they started their business.

It is downright scary. So how do you separate yourself from the pack and **ensure** that you and your business don't become one of these statistics?

I have said it already, but it bears repeating. There is a huge difference between mastering your craft and mastering how to grow a profitable business; you need to do both. If you are struggling to grow your business in a profitable, sustainable way, the reason is simple: There is something you don't know or haven't learned yet that you need to. This is why I am such a huge advocate of getting coaching and mentoring from someone who is doing what you want to do at the level at which you want to do it. Keep it simple; let someone else's mistakes and learnings be your opportunity.

The Five Keys to High Six- and Seven-Figure Success

There are five key ingredients that I find repeatedly in the businesses that achieve high six- and seven-figure success: mastery of the basics, modeling, mentorship, emphasis on profit-producing activities coupled with tracking and measurement, and a focus on teambuilding or outsourcing.

1. Mastery of the basics (infrastructure)

There are five key pillars that you must have in place to build and grow a sustainable business:

- Sales: direct interaction with prospects in which leads convert to sales.
- Marketing: visibility, nurturing, publicity, public relations. This can takes thousands of different forms. It is where you generate leads and bring them through the know, like, and trust process.
- Service: delivering your product or service exceptionally well leading to upsells, referrals, lifetime customers, and increased spending.
- Operations: financial management, proper recordkeeping, infrastructure, systems, processes, etc.
- Team: The right people, expertise and support resources needed to execute your vision.

Everything else falls under one of these four categories. Most businesses that fail are out of alignment in one of these five areas.

When you look at the basics, you need to evaluate things like pricing, messaging, visibility, and your conversion strategy for the visibility that you do have. Connecting these dots allows a business to capitalize on the resources that they have and leveraging them to produce significantly more profit.

Pricing your business effectively is a core component of building wealth and achieving lifestyle freedom. Nine out of ten clients who come to me need to close to double their rates and completely reframe how they are selling their products and services. I get a lot of pushback on this from nearly every single client. Once I finally get them to implement the changes and raise their rates, overnight they can work far fewer hours for significantly more income.

Many businesses fail because they are not able to close enough sales at a profitable enough price point to work reasonable hours and keep the business going. A big mistake that entrepreneurs make when pricing their business is that they calculate their hourly rate assuming they will be working at this rate for the majority of their working hours. Not so.

You will spend more than 80 percent of your time on activities outside of servicing your customers. This means that you need to look at the other 20 percent of your time to determine how much you need to be making for those hours in order to achieve your goals. This is also why scale is so important because there is a limit to what you personally can do.

I want you to pause here to do a quick assessment of how well you are pricing your business and determine if it's time to make some changes now. Failure to do so may very well leave you among those scary statistics.

Ask yourself these questions:

- *When was the last time you increased prices?*
- *In which percentile are you priced compared to your competitors (e.g. 50 percent higher, 50 percent lower, etc.)?*
- *How much is your time worth? How many hours of the week do you spend on activities that yield this hourly rate?*
- *Do you know what you need to be earning hourly to achieve your income goals?*
- *How can you design a new product or service that allows you to charge rates in line with your income goal?*

_____

_____

_____

_____

_____

_____

_____

2. Modeling

Success leaves clues! Modeling is a critical component when you are building a solid foundation for your business. Find someone or an organization that is doing what you want to do at the level at which you want to do it and begin studying their strategy and their pillars for success.

There are many ways to benefit from thousands of hours and dollars already spent on testing, research, and implementation by other organizations already established in your space. Simply put: Don't reinvent the wheel!

Modeling can cut years off your timeline for success, but it does not mean you should try to be anything other than who you truly are. You never want to model another business to the point at which you are second best at being someone else rather than being the absolute best at who you truly are.

3. Mentorship, outside council, and coaching

Every top performer, athletic superstar, or leading-edge CEO has outside council in many forms. It is critical to get mentorship, training, coaching, and support to get from where you are to where you need to be.

It is not a luxury but a necessity if you want to break out of the status quo and achieve something extraordinary. You will be hard pressed to find anyone performing and producing at the level you desire who does not have coaches, mentors, and advisors guiding them every step of the way. Do not go at it alone; it is a recipe for failure because you simply do not have all of the perspective, knowledge, and experience that can only be achieved by and through the process of building your business.

4. Heavy emphasis on sales/profit-producing activities coupled with tracking and measuring results

I work with individuals and organizations across countless industries in businesses of all shapes and sizes. I will tell you with certainty that those who succeed and profit long term live by these things:

- What you focus on expands
- What you measure gets done
- A plan or goal without accountability is wishful thinking
- Inspect what you expect or prepare to be disappointed

The other thing I find is that those who thrive have a laser-beam focus on profit-producing activities. They know what works, and they work tirelessly to expand and replicate it.

Entrepreneurs and business owners who want to build true wealth understand that sales and marketing are the lifeblood of their businesses and commit to working on these two areas continually no matter how foreign or uncomfortable it may make them feel.

I many times find that the businesses that struggle simply do not track, measure, and hold their teams or themselves accountable for the things that matter most.

5. Focus on teambuilding, outsourcing, and delegation

Are you a super employee or CEO?

Are you a visionary leader or master of the never-ending to-do list?

You cannot be both of these things and do them both well.

I constantly hear small business owners complain about how hard it is to build a team, relinquish control, and get others to perform at a satisfactory level. This attitude is a great way to run yourself and your business right into the ground. Yes, there are challenges that come with building a team and there always will be.

Anything – and I mean anything – of consequence, value, or meaning in this life takes work and is not without challenges. Otherwise, everyone would be a millionaire, in perfect health and physical form, with perfect relationships, doing only what they desire in life.

If you are serious about building wealth, freedom, and ongoing success, you must learn how to delegate, get results through others, and let go of the tasks that are below your pay grade.

If you master these five areas, you will *thrive*. Yes, you do deserve financial abundance, freedom, and fulfillment. You can have it all, but your actions, focus, and day-to-day behaviors must align with the outcomes you want to achieve.

Again, I want to emphasize that there is a difference between mastering your craft and building your business. Unfortunately, gone are the days in which being the best at what you do will earn you a living. To build a booming business, you have to master how to grow your business. Just because you build it does not mean they will come. That means one of your most important focus areas must be on learning how to attract, convert, and retain high-paying customers for your business. Keep that difference in mind and don't get caught in the entitlement trap of assuming the customers will arrive at your doorstep through osmosis.

Take some time now to really reflect on these ideas:

Which of the principles that we discussed in this chapter do you need to take action on right away?

_____

_____

_____

_____

Do you have at least one entrepreneurial venture or business you are building to grow your income and create multiple streams of income?

_____

_____

_____

_____

What are you doing right now to sharpen your business skill set?

_____

_____

_____

_____

What investments in your own learning, training, development, or growth do you need to act on to gain the knowledge you need to achieve the level of success you desire?

_____

_____

_____

_____

Keep in mind that you don't need to have all the knowledge or answers; you simply need to assemble the right support system, training, and resources to help you get there.

If you are just getting started launching your own business and don't know where to begin or have been in business for a while but are stuck, begin to research business-building programs and coaches such as myself that specialize in this specific area. All you have to do is be willing and get yourself in the game. There are resources out there to help you with all the rest.

Recap:

➢ What you think of as a detriment or hardship is very likely a blessing. Change your perspective.

➢ Unless you are willing to hustle and stop simply showing up and clocking in, nothing will change. You must be the one to shake things up and set things on fire in order to achieve what you want in life.

➢ Without at least one six-figure business, you are leaving your future... and very likely your family's well-being... to chance or to the whim of someone else.

➢ You must understand the basic principles of business or you will become another business-failure statistic.

➢ Business mastery includes five ingredients:

   o Mastery of the basics (sales, marketing, service, and operations)

   o Modeling: don't reinvent the wheel, model it

   o Mentorship: don't go it alone

   o Profit-producing activities coupled with the ability to track and measure

   o Teambuilding or outsourcing: you cannot do it all yourself and create a successful business.

Most entrepreneurs and leaders who want a certain lifestyle and financial freedom have the passion and the craft but not the mastery of sales and marketing… that's exactly why so many businesses fail.

To learn the competencies that are necessary to create your next six-figure breakthrough and beyond, visit <u>KellyRoachCoaching.com/guide</u> and sign up for the free book guide.

6

INVEST IN YOURSELF DAILY

As you move up the corporate ladder, you take on more and more until you are at your breaking point. I was running 17 branches, breaking company records, achieving results no one had ever fathomed with my team, yet I felt completely empty. Outwardly, I had achieved my dream: I was in my 20s, meeting CEOs in boardrooms, and training hundreds of individuals how to be successful based on my achievements, but on the inside, my heart hurt.

It's very hard to come to terms with the fact that many times you get exactly what you want in life only to realize that it is not what will bring you happiness and fulfillment after all.

For me, I learned that outward success was not enough. A big job and important title didn't do it for me – I knew there was more. I was unhappy... extremely unhappy. I had sacrificed relationships, time with family, and overall just being present in life for years.

When you work for someone else, you live and die by their rulebook. You are there to serve on behalf of your employer, and your job is to make them money, on their terms, and to do it "their way," or get the hell out.

I hear a lot of people complain about their jobs. They hate their boss, can't stand the company they work for, think what they are required to do every day is ridiculous, and the list goes on.

Any of this sound familiar to you?

NEWS FLASH! We possess free will. We all have the ability at any given moment to make a decision, create a change in our lives, and get started on a new path.

I knew I needed to make a change, a big one. I knew that success without fulfillment would not equal happiness. I also knew that I wanted freedom in my life and to make income in the millions, not hundreds of thousands. The solution was obvious but certainly not easy. I had worked for the better part of a decade to get to where I was and had literally given everything I had to being successful in my role, yet I knew I needed a new path forward.

This meant starting over from zero. The only way to achieve my top three values of freedom, financial abundance, and fulfillment was through starting my own business that focused on helping others succeed.

To me, personal growth is essential to happiness because happiness at its heart comes from forward progress.

> *There was no other option. In my heart, I knew this was my calling.*

Think about the happiest times of your life. Chances are you were doing something you loved, experiencing success doing it, and getting some type of positive feedback in that area. It could be a time of life, an event, a relationship, or a career. It all comes back to you feeling like you are on the right path, a path that is authentic to who you really are and one that feeds your soul.

Everything Begins (and Ends!) Between Your Ears

One important take away from this chapter that I hope will really stick with you is that you have to be the hero of your own life... because no one else will be. You are not a victim, and no matter what has happened in the past, you and only you are the decider of your future.

It takes work. It's not easy to face your fears, make a big decision, take action even when you are unsure. It is, however, necessary if you want to live a full, happy, and fulfilled life. Your journey is yours alone, so it is critical to release the need to be a pleaser to everyone around you and get focused on the work you need to do to get from where you are to where you want to be.

Much of what we have talked about in this book so far relates to the actions, behaviors, and decisions necessary to achieve unstoppable success. I want to bring your focus to the fact that everything begins between your ears. If you do not work at growing as a person and evolving your way of thinking, no matter how much you may want things to be different in your life, they will stay very much the same or even get worse as they compound over time.

It takes honesty and accountability to assess what you don't like about your life and most importantly what you need to do to change it. When I work with my life coaching clients, I find they have spent countless hours analyzing, stressing, experiencing anxiety around the things with which they are struggling, but barely a moment on the plan, actions, and outcomes they want to create.

I'll share a quick story to illustrate how great we are at attracting *exactly* what we don't want:

Growing up with five kids in our family naturally we had the biggest, ugliest station wagon you can ever imagine, complete with wood paneling on the sides. It was embarrassing as all get out, and I did everything possible to avoid being seen entering or exiting whenever possible (as any kid would). As my 16th birthday approached, I had saved a few thousand dollars to buy my first car. As you can surmise, a few thousand dollars didn't get me very far and the selection was pretty grim. I needed a car because I worked a lot, had tons of after school activities, and my mom was about to lose it running me all over town. All I could think about every day was how excited I was to not have to ride in the station wagon anymore and how much I hated station wagons and how I would *never* drive a station wagon....

> *You can attract exactly what you do NOT want by making it the center of your focus.*

When the time came to buy a car, my dad was pretty strict and would only let me buy from a few people he knew locally that he trusted since the car was going to be old and run down to start. Well don't you know, the only thing available in my price range was an ugly red station wagon. So I had a choice: either wait around for something else or get my first taste of freedom in my own car. You can guess how the rest of the story went. And yes, I'd done a superb job of attracting exactly what I didn't want.

We are so good at focusing on what we don't want that many times we attract exactly that right into our lives. It's why people run through cycles of the same issues in their lives repeatedly. That is where they fixate. What you focus on expands and where your focus goes energy flows.

There were a lot of lessons in this for me even beyond the lesson of attracting what I didn't want by focusing too much on it. A big lesson was that I planned poorly. Had I saved more money, I would have had more options; had I started looking sooner, I could have waited to find something ideal versus jumping on the only thing available when I "needed" a car.

Take a few minutes having read about my experience of attracting the very thing I didn't want to focus on similar events in your own life:

How has poor planning prevented you from getting what you really wanted?

Can you think of a time where you put more thought and energy into what you didn't want rather than planning and taking action on what you did?

Have there been times where your options have been severely limited by your own doing?

Your Interconnected Life

Things change no matter what. Whether things change for the better is totally up to you. A critical piece of maturing as a person is investing in your own growth. This is about much more than business, your career, or income. Every area of life is interconnected, so evolving on all fronts is critical. Many times we get so focused on one area that we let the others slip and end up with severe, unintended consequences.

Take a look at these examples and reflect on how these could relate to your own life:

- A father and husband is fiercely committed to his family and determined to provide a comfortable life for them. He works two jobs often leaving the house at 5:00 in the morning and not getting home until 7:00 or 8:00 at night. His wife becomes increasingly dissatisfied with his lack of interest and involvement in their home life and is sick of raising the kids alone. Finally, she files for divorce and wants to begin a new life rather than feeling unimportant and alone even while in a "marriage." This father – who sacrificed seeing his kids grow up, gave everything he had to give them a good life, and allow his wife to be home with the kids – lost everything and ended up alone even though he spent his whole life working to give his family a good life and take care of his wife whom he loved.

I am sure everyone reading this scenario can think of someone they know who has gone through something similar or in the same realm.

Was either wrong? How did this happen? What could have been done to prevent this? How can this be a lesson in your own life?

- A mother had a horrible childhood and struggled immensely with the fact that she never had a relationship with her own mother. She committed that she would dedicate her whole life to being the best mother she could be. Her children were her world, her whole focus, and she wanted so badly to be loved by them that she smothered them, wanting to be involved with every aspect of their lives. In turn, her children resented her for being overbearing and too clingy to the point of it inhibiting their growth and development. Her children ended up intentionally moving away from home as soon as they could and keeping a spotty, distant relationship with their mother so as to try to create healthy boundaries.

What went wrong here? Is it possible that despite only good intentions this loving mother completely alienated her children and pushed them away? What do you think was missing?

It's All about Balance

Balance is key. Sometimes we get so determined, so focused on one thing we want so desperately, we risk everything else in our life to get it – even if that risk is completely unintentional. Personal development is largely about growing into your higher self: gaining more perspective, self-awareness, and emotional maturity.

A lifelong commitment to growth and learning allows you to evolve and achieve results in any area of life at an accelerated rate. Identifying the key areas that need to be incorporated into your daily rituals or overall life plan will help you look at your life from a 50,000-foot view rather than making decisions in the moment or based on emotion.

Here are some areas to consider when you design your daily rituals for growth:

- Family
- Personal fulfillment
- Health and wellness/fitness
- Nutrition
- Career/wealth building
- Spirituality
- Community

You may rank these differently than your spouse or the person sitting right next to you, and of course, there is no right or wrong. The point is that if your life is one dimensional, eventually the very thing you are working the hardest for will be taken away… just as it was for the father and mother in the previous scenarios. In each of those cases, the answer to "What went wrong?" was a lack of balance and the inability to avoid making decisions based on emotion or in the moment. There was definitely a lack of trying to view the situations from 50,000 feet.

The best example that I personally see and experience every day are the average Americans who kill themselves working hard, sacrificing greatly to "save for retirement," and "buy their beach house" (or some similar tangible goal). While they are working this plan, they are eating crap, not taking care of their bodies, spending little to no time with their families. And in the end what do you have? A lonely, obese, disease-ridden person who can buy the beach house but is too sick, depressed and overweight to enjoy it.

Daily rituals help me maintain balance in the areas that I believe are key to my growth and happiness as a person. Here are some of the daily rituals that I live by:

- The first thing I do every day is a gratitude meditation.
- I either listen to or read something that will help me grow (spiritually, in business, or related to personal growth) every day.
- I integrate exercise into my workday daily when possible. Usually this means walking outside and reconnecting with nature while I am on phone calls for at least 30 minutes a day.
- I always have a glass of water sitting by my side and drink at least eight glasses a day.
- I get eight hours of sleep a night pretty much without question. I limit my exposure to toxic people, television, and interactions.
- Family comes first. There is work time and there is family time, and when it's family time, I am 1000% present and focused. Everything that I work for is for my family so we can build a wonderful life together. My husband is my confidant and my best friend, and my daughter is my everything. Anytime I make a decision, I ask myself whether what I am doing is beneficial or detrimental to my relationships and family dynamic. This includes limiting travel and working many hours after Madison is asleep and before Billy and Madison are awake in the morning.

What are your five daily rituals for growth and balance in your life?

1. _____

2. _____

3. _____

4. _____

5. _____

Are there any new rituals you want to add into your daily routine?

Do you do something every day to help you grow?

To bring everything we discussed in this chapter together, I want to finish with this: Starting and growing your own business will be the greatest personal growth exercise on which you will ever embark. It will require you to come face-to-face with your fears and weaknesses. Don't run from the things that you fear. Most of the time, the very thing that you most resist will unlock everything you have been struggling to achieve.

Whether it's public speaking, selling, writing, or even just proclaiming your goals and dreams to your family and friends, it is okay to be fearful, but you need to do it anyway. You have to find a way to push through the emotions and take the action if you want to arrive at your destination.

Staying in your comfort zone puts you in a tiny box and forces you to live within those confines. While it may be more comfortable and less risky, you will never achieve your true potential this way.

Everything is waiting for you. Your time is now! It's time to push past the boundaries of the past, shatter your own glass ceiling, and take your life to the next level in every area.

Recap:

➢ Making space for all of the "big rocks" in your life is critical. Balance is tough but attempt to do your best given your personal circumstances.

➢ You have free will; therefore, you have the ability to change your life and get started on a new path.

➢ You are happiest when you are on a path that is authentic to who you really are and one that feeds your soul.

➢ Make the choice to be the hero of your own story not the victim of someone else's.

➢ That which you focus on, you attract. Do not focus on what you don't want.

➢ Every area of your life is interconnected; you must evolve on all fronts.

➢ Create your own rituals for growth.

➢ Face your fear and go for it!

Have you started tuning in to Unstoppable Success Radio yet? It's my totally FREE, easily accessible radio show hosted on iTunes and Sticher™ radio that is all about helping you achieve a higher level of success in business and in life. This one small step can begin a massive transformation in your life. Grab your phone or tablet and subscribe to Unstoppable Success Radio today!

PART 3:
UNSTOPPABLE
SUCCESS

CHAPTER

7

SALES

If you learn to sell, you will always have security.

When the crash happened in 2008, thousands of people were laid off, let go, or terminated due to their companies' instability and slow down. I was working in the staffing industry at the forefront of the employment market, and we were hit hard. I watched our competitors shut down offices, and my own company let many individuals go.

I was in my mid-twenties, and I held in my hands the careers and livelihoods of 30 plus other professionals. I will be forever proud of the jobs that were preserved and the people's careers that were saved because of the sales training I was able to give my staff.

I worked tirelessly day in and day out to train my team to have killer sales instincts and to go out and close. When the stakes were high and we needed to perform, we did, despite the market collapsing around us. Not only did we perform, but we broke company records that year and stayed incredibly profitable while keeping our team intact. Like I said, a sales skill equals security.

While sales alone was not enough, it had a lot to do with our ability to overcome an incredibly difficult situation. We also had to adapt to the market, change our focus and create an innovative approach to the market conditions. Maybe most importantly, I had to give the team confidence and guidance, so we could overcome the challenges we were facing and succeed.

Successful entrepreneurs, business owners, and corporate executives understand the importance of sales to any business's success. It doesn't have to be your favorite thing or even a key skillset, but you do need to understand its importance and, if nothing else, build a team around you that is successful in this area. At some point in this crazy world, "sales" became a dirty word. People want the results of it but at the same time want nothing to do with it … explain to me that riddle?

Great sales people are made not born (I think the quote goes), and it couldn't be more true. Becoming a top sales producer is a choice. There are specific steps, strategies, and processes that will take you from amateur to pro… no matter how horrible you think you are at sales. When I train entrepreneurs and companies big and small how to radically increase their sales and profits, much of the work we do is in the structure, set-up, and strategy. The selling itself is a piece of cake once you understand the mindset and mechanics involved.

You can become an invaluable leader, unstoppable entrepreneur, and highly successful business owner if you are willing to step out of your comfort zone and make it your mission to excel in this area. No matter what you set out to do, developing your sales skill set will help you get there faster, easier, and with more confidence, guaranteed.

If you are interested in:

- Financial freedom…
- Unlimited earning potential…

- Insulation from the economy…
- Development of a transferrable and invaluable skill set that can be used in any industry, organization, or your own business to achieve magnificent success…

… then I recommend committing to lifelong education in sales!

Redefining "Sales"

What I most want to drive home to you is that sales is, without a doubt, the cornerstone of success. When you hear "sales," you may be immediately thinking used car salesperson. Or hawker on an infomercial. You would not be alone in that reaction. Admittedly, that is a stereotype of sales, but it's not the one you should be thinking of. In all likelihood, that stereotypical image makes you cringe (and with good reason!)… and leads to the typical negative reaction to the thought of sales.

Instead, I want to shift your mindset to a new definition and new way to look at sales: Sales is a transfer of inspiration. It's the moment at which your passion, your fire, and your compelling message hits the other person, and they do the very thing you want them to do for their own reasons. The result becomes a win-win situation for you both.

Ultimately, sales speaks not only to a monetary transfer for a product or service, it also addresses what leadership is truly all about. It's about getting results through others; it's about getting investors for your business; it's about getting your "A-Team" that will push your business and mission in the world forward; it's about getting people to support you and do things for you; it's about your ability to communicate your vision in such a compelling way that others work as hard for your dream as you do.

Very simply, sales touches every facet of business and financial success. If you want to be the CEO of your business and life, you must get your brain wrapped around this concept and embrace it.

Otherwise, you will be relegated to being the person on the hamster wheel, working as hard as you can day in and day out for a fraction of your true value.

This concept is the only way to get your message and your mission to come full circle. Remember, as I mentioned previously, even the top sales producer can only achieve so much alone. It's through the teamwork, collaboration, and alliance of others that you can achieve true success.

Most business owners have the dream of getting to the million-dollar mark in their businesses. It's a common objective. The single one thing that I see that holds people back from achieving this goal is… sales. For some reason, with the rise of the Internet and online marketing, people confuse the difference between sales and marketing. They are distinct entities.

In fact, it is the marriage of sales and marketing – these two distinct entities working in unison – that creates a spontaneous combustion and explosion of profit in your business. Almost 99 percent of business owners miss the opportunities before them because they run screaming from the word "sales."

> *"Sales are contingent upon the attitude of the salesman – not the attitude of the prospect."*
>
> ~ W. Clement Stone

Not every person is a natural born sales person. Most of the best sales people I've worked with, trained, coached, or managed, had no sales experience whatsoever. It was in their mindset and mentality that allowed them to succeed and achieve. The most successful people in the world are those who fight for their dream and realize that if they aren't advocating for the results they want and aren't screaming from the rooftops what they know they deserve, they will end up down in the valley with everyone else rather than reaching the apex of success.

What Is the Missing Link?

I want to impress upon you the importance of wrapping your head and heart around sales as the cornerstone of business and financial success. I cannot begin to train you on the sales process in this chapter or even in this book. That topic is a book in and of itself. I simply want you to understand that the missing link in getting your beach house, in retiring ten years early, in your boat purchase, in paying off your mortgage early, and in paying your kids' college tuitions very likely falls in the realm of lack of a sales skill set.

Sales simplified comes down to your ability to influence others in such a way that both you and they ultimately get what you want. Think about all the areas of life in which this applies: family, community, career, business, finances. It literally touches on every area of life.

As a business owner, it's not simply a matter of you getting out and selling a product or service. Remember, even the top producer can only sell so much. It's a matter of your work as a sales leader, visionary, and coach coupled with a sales model that works combined with an incredible marketing program. If you don't have these things working in concert with each other, that is your missing link to what you want to achieve.

Sales are not simply transactions – dollars and cents. Sales are about your ability to move others rapidly and aggressively in the direction needed to achieve your goals. We're talking about the ability to influence others to do what you want them to do *for their own reasons*. When it is for their own reasons, they will work and fight as hard as you do to reach your goal. The stronger you get in your ability to communicate and leverage this in your business and career, the sooner you can skyrocket your sales and profit.

It's critical to understand that the thing that you resist most in your business and the thing that you resist most in your life is most likely the ultimate key to get everything you want that you've never been able to achieve. In my experience, for nine out of ten entrepreneurs, that resistance is selling... transferring inspiration to others to get them to move willingly in the direction of the goal. Things like multi-million-dollar contracts, upfront payments, closing clients who are the perfect and profitable fit for your business all lie in your ability to sell.

Confidence and certainty play a big role in this as well as power in yourself and your ability to empower others.

> *Most business success stories start with going door to door, pounding the pavement, or making calls from the kitchen table or garage to get from "no" to "yes."*

What do you need to do today to improve your selling skill set? I coach daily about sales and help companies put the processes in place that they need. I'll assert that I understand sales and the selling process as well as anyone, yet I still continue to regularly put myself through sales training in order to continue upping my game both for my own company and those that I coach.

Have you embraced the core regarding how you make money in your business or career? If you haven't embraced sales as a core component of how to achieve your dream, chances are you never will achieve them.

How will you ever get a team of advocates (and remember, no one does it alone), if you are running screaming from sales? Is sales a part of your culture, something that you embrace daily and passionately? It is what will take you from where you are to where you want to be.

One of the key reasons to embrace sales as an entrepreneur or small business owner is not because you will necessarily be the one selling but because it is very hard to teach something you don't understand. Invest in yourself, so you can hire, train, and develop others to do the selling for you.

If you have a team, ensure you are using daily tracking, measurements, and accountabilities to drive results. This is the second place in which I often see business owners leaving money on the table: the lack of tracking, management, and accountability.

Businesses leave millions of dollars on the table because of laziness and an unwillingness to do the work to create and follow through in these critical areas.

Do you have these elements in place and are you doing everything you can do to build, develop, and grow your sales team?

Finally, ask yourself how you can take this to the next level? Is it at the sales producer level, sales management level, or your CEO level? How are you making your team better and empowering them to sell more on your behalf?

Sales and Marketing Are Not Interchangeable!

Too many business owners want to replace selling with marketing. Marketing is a huge part of my own business; however, the explosion of growth has come from the marriage of sales and marketing. They are two sides of the same coin. You must understand how these work together: Marketing gets you the warm leads and expressed interest, but sales is the transfer of inspiration to close the deal.

Yes, some people will buy by clicking a button on your site, from an audio or video, or as a result of getting an email. But you are going to work so much harder for far less money if all of your efforts are in marketing. You can work incessantly to build a list of thousands, but you can make *ten times the money with far less effort* with a balance of email marketing catapulted by utilizing traditional sales. Which one of these approaches sounds more logical?

Chances are mismanagement or lack of outside sales is having a tremendously negative effect on your bottom line and your overall success.

What do I see that the most successful entrepreneurs have in common? The ones who are easily making six and seven figures? The ones who experience incredible year-over-year growth? The answer and most important thing is imperfect action – taking action every day and understanding that a prospect is giving you nothing unless you are following up and doing everything you can do to convert them from prospect to client.

Taking action every day with your prospects keeps you top of mind, so when they *are* ready to reach out with their need, they think of you. People are looking for shortcuts and the easy way out, but in reality, it's these people who market their businesses like crazy with little to no results.

Your Solution Is Right in Front of You… Now!

I suspect that right now you have enough prospects and leads sitting in your business *now* to create your next six-figure breakthrough in the next six months. You may be shaking your head in disbelief at that assertion because you are struggling to create that six-figure business (and life) that you want, and you're the one on the hamster wheel running like crazy but not really getting anywhere. You may also be thinking if it were that easy, you would already be doing it. I make that assertion because I've seen it repeatedly with my coaching clients. Chances are that you are just like them and making the very same mistake: You are chasing new leads rather than focusing on the ones right under your nose at this moment.

I am so certain of this that I recently created an entire training series walking entrepreneurs through how they can quickly and easily add an extra $100,000 in sales in their business in the next six months without getting a single new lead. I literally am breaking down the exact play by play of how we did this and how you can, too, because it is so simple, yet no one is doing it. You can access the training for free now by visiting this link: www.kellyroachcoaching.com.

Frequency and consistency out pull all other metrics in sales, so if you simply increase these two areas with the current and past customers and warm leads you already have in your business, you will start to see some drastic results pretty quickly.

Take some time now to audit your level of proficiency in these key areas that impact your ability to achieve financial abundance, freedom, and unstoppable success:

1. *Are you effective at getting others to purchase your products or services?*

2. *As the CEO of your business, are you an impactful sales leader?*

3. *Do you get peak performance from the individuals responsible for selling your products and services?*

4. *Does your communication with others convey your message in a compelling and effective way?*

5. *How well do you build alliances, affiliations, and strategic partners in business?*

6. *How well do you make connections and network with centers of influence that can help move your mission forward?*

On a scale of 1 to 10, how well have you mastered the transfer of inspiration in everything that you do?

_____

_____

_____

_____

_____

What can you start doing right away to improve your ability to use sales to grow your income and achieve your dreams?

_____

_____

_____

_____

_____

As a final note: strategy, mechanics, and the process of selling is a deep, broad topic, certainly too much to cover here. If you need in-depth training, resources, and support in this area, simply email my team at customersupport@kellyroachcoaching.com and ask about the resources, training, coaching, and consulting we provide in this area.

Recap:

> Sales equals security whether you are building your business or advancing your career.

> Sales is not simply a monetary transfer for the goods and services you provide. It is the transfer of inspiration to get others to do what you want them to do for their own reasons.

> If you want to achieve everything you dream, you must embrace the thing you are resisting most. For many, that thing is sales.

> It bears repeating: You cannot do it alone. Even the top sales producers have a limit to what they can achieve by themselves.

> Sales and marketing are not interchangeable. They are two sides of the same coin. Success comes from the marriage between them.

> Take action every day on your prospects. You will achieve more with less effort by focusing on your existing good prospects than by working harder than you need to chase more prospects and trying to build a list of thousands.

> Sales training is ongoing. The best of the best understand this and are always improving their sales skill set.

The power to influence and move an audience is critical if you want to build a scalable business. Sales is at the heart of everything you do as a business leader and entrepreneur. If you have not mastered sales yet but realize that this is the next step for you, visit KellyRoachCoaching.com/guide *and sign up for the free book guide.*

CHAPTER

8

DISCIPLINE

The most powerful personal characteristic on Earth? Discipline.

I set out to achieve a very specific result in my corporate career, and success resulted from blood, sweat, and tears (aka discipline). I sacrificed immensely to achieve it. There were many days I wanted to quit. I experienced every possible challenge, struggle, and setback you could possibly imagine. Beyond the business challenges on my journey, my entire world was turned upside down continually with family crises. My mom nearly died from a sudden, massive blood clot, and my dad fell ill needing me to shut his business down and attend to his personal affairs and the list goes on.... To say that it took discipline to stay the course would be an understatement.

> *No matter what your circumstances are today, if you exert enough discipline, anything is possible. With enough discipline, you can have, be, or do anything you want.*

The bottom line is that if you are alive, you will deal with shit, a lot of it. Discipline is the personal power to rise above the circumstances at hand, no matter how challenging, and keep moving forward.

Why did I endure these things and stay the course? Absolute clarity around what I wanted in my life. I knew a few years into my working career that I would not be able to achieve my income and life goals working for anyone other than myself. I also knew that the best way to get the education, experience, and income needed to launch my dream was to stay strong and keep moving forward on the path I was on. For years even after this realization, I gave 1000 percent to performing at the highest level possible in my job while getting up early and staying up late to build my dream business.

My story is only a single example. Anyone who's achieved success in their various fields did it by discipline and by staying the course to achieve their dream when others didn't believe it was possible. Consider these examples:

- Stephen King's first novel, *Carrie*, was rejected consistently before being published. Staying the course, his books have now sold over 350 million copies. He's undoubtedly successful.

- Michael Jordan was cut from his high school basketball team. He went on to be a six-time NBA Champion, five-time NBA MVP, three-time NBA All-Star. I'm not sure how you define success, but if the statistics he racked up don't spell S-U-C-C-E-S-S, nothing does.

- Steven Spielberg could not get into the film school of his choice: University of Southern California School of Theater, Film and Television, being rejected three times. He attended another school and went on to collect Oscars, Golden Globes, and Emmys. His list of awards goes on for pages, and that says nothing of the commercial success of his work.

- Walt Disney was fired from his newspaper job because he "lacked imagination and had no good ideas." You have no doubt enjoyed at least one of his movies, television shows, or theme parks at one time. If you're like most people, that enjoyment is expansive. We can all be glad that Disney had enough discipline and belief in his ideas to see them through! We have all been beneficiaries.

The good news is that you already have the power and control to develop the characteristic of discipline. How do I know that? Because *everyone* has this ability.

Almost every client asks, "What do I need to do to create a breakthrough? To get to the next level? How come I'm working as hard as I can but seem to keep spinning my wheels, getting nowhere?"

The truth is, you can work incredibly hard at all the wrong things because you are avoiding what is necessary to get to where you want to be. And that sums up my personal definition of discipline: Doing what you need to do when you don't feel like doing it.

The most successful people in any field are never the smartest, most talented, with the most money or resources, or with the most innovative, novel ideas. It is the people with the personal power of discipline to do what's necessary to achieve their personal goals. If Stephen King, Michael Jordan, Steven Spielberg, or Walt Disney didn't have discipline to keep trying in the face of challenges and rejection, none of us would know their names. Discipline drove their respective successes.

More than 90 percent of the time, we work on what comes easily and naturally; we work on what keeps us in that box in which we feel safe. What we really need to do is that one thing that we will do everything in the world to avoid. My coaching clients always start by telling me: "I'm just not good at sales," "I'm just not good at managing people," or "I'm just not good at public speaking."

Success and fulfillment aren't derived from whether or not you're good at something. It's about making the decision moment-by-moment that keeps you on your path toward your highest good and the ultimate outcomes you are trying to achieve.

I'm going to share very specific examples of situations in which discipline really comes into play, and I encourage you to take notes as you're reading and evaluate if you've been a culprit of lack of discipline in these areas. Challenge yourself and ask if you are really doing what you need to be doing. Chances are the answer will be "no."

> *"We must all suffer one of two things: the pain of discipline or the pain of regret and disappointment."*
>
> ~ *Jim Rohn*

The good news is that making a change is simple; the bad news is that it is uncomfortable. You've spent your entire life spinning a web of excuses and creating barriers that have kept you safe and from doing the one thing that you need to. It may be caused by habit, fatigue, or feeling overwhelmed. There are a million reasons we don't do what needs to be done, but that doesn't make it okay. You are the only one with the power and control to change the direction of your life.

Income

To grow your income, certain things are needed: correct pricing, interaction with customers, daily work to be a premium provider of your product or service, and negotiations and persuasions that may be uncomfortable. (And I think I already mentioned a few times: start your own business!)

When I come across an individual who cannot grow their income, the problem stems from a lack of discipline to complete the profit-producing activities needed to achieve their goals... period.

Look at your own income. Look in the mirror and ask: "What is really holding me back from achieving my income goals? What have I not been willing to do? What is standing in my way?"

Chances are you haven't calculated the compounding factors of what it really takes to grow your income. Days, weeks, and months – maybe years – are slipping by, and your passion and flame might be starting to flicker and dwindle. You need to assess what small daily actions you have been avoiding or even blatantly refusing to do.

Relationships

Next, evaluate your relationships. Everyone has a lot on their plates, and there are multi-faceted responsibilities with business, career, life, kids... and the list goes on. I don't know anyone who has a simple situation, one without daily responsibilities and stress.

To get the relationship you really want with your spouse, significant other, family, friends and colleagues, ask yourself who *you* really need to be. What do you need to give that you haven't been giving? Have you been expecting to get something out of the relationship that you haven't asked for or that you haven't reciprocated?

For example, when you're stressed or frustrated, do you blame others or project that on to others? Do you have a bit of a freak out and then feel guilty about what you said or did? That's a lack of discipline. You need to be clear about who you want to be, who you want to be with as well as having clarity about what you want the relationship to look and feel like.

You have to be that person and be authentically aligned with who that person is. Stress and the factors that weigh on us can make this very difficult. Are you bringing these outside elements into the relationship that could be destroying it?

Employee Performance

Perhaps you haven't even hired an employee yet. What is holding you back? Are you so afraid or do you lack enough trust in yourself that you don't have the discipline to take the actions needed to grow your business and income by hiring an employee or contractor?

If you find yourself in this situation, let me be blunt: It is not okay. You must be willing to step up to the plate and be accountable to yourself and others to do what's necessary to grow your business,

> *Discipline is doing what needs to be done when you don't feel like doing it.*

so you can afford to hire and expand. Remember: You can't do it alone.

On the other hand, I often see those with employees who let them go on for months or years without putting profit on the bottom line. They fail to do what's needed from a leadership or management standpoint to make employees successful and get their return on the investment they made in these people.

In terms of employee performance, this means inspecting what you expect. Dig into the details of what employees are producing in relation to their goals. Hold people accountable!

Discipline means training rather than doing it yourself. Go ahead and underline or highlight that sentence. I see it repeatedly with clients; I have to force them to go back and train and delegate. You have to get over the mindset of: It's faster and easier to do it myself. It is not. At least not if you want to grow your business and income. All that mindset does is dig the hole deeper with you stuck in it as the super employee, the hamster on the wheel instead of a true CEO and business owner.

Your employees will never be more successful than you set them up to be through the road map you give them and the training you provide. An employee's performance and ability to succeed depend more on the manager and leader (you!) than it does on them. A good leader can take a mediocre talent and make them successful with the right systems and strategies in place coupled with a well-oiled training approach.

Kids

Let's face it: at the end of the day, you're spent. If you're a parent, are you sending the message that you want to send if you are relying on television and toys? Are you sending the message you want to send if you are giving in to every tantrum and whim because you're tired and want to stop the crying? Or are you truly a disciplined, empowered parent teaching your kids what you truly want them to learn?

Taking the extra step to avoid caving in and taking the easy way out to make it better for you in the moment pays off in the long term. Yes, it's a difficult step, but if you avoid it, you will find yourself in a repeating cycle and habit that is much harder to break in the future.

Health and Wellness

We all know that you are what you eat, and if we put crap in our bodies, we are not going to feel and look good and will pay for it later. Weigh your goal (no pun intended) of looking and feeling good and maintaining overall good health against the instant gratification of what might taste good right now… or what's fast and easy to eat.

For many business owners and entrepreneurs, they're juggling so many balls and keeping so many plates spinning that they bail out and choose what is fast and easy because they need to grab something now or don't have time to cook. There are things you can do to avoid this: Get groceries delivered, hire someone to cook, stock your refrigerator and freezer weekly with healthy snacks and meals (do the same with the work fridge and freezer).

> *"It was character that got us out of bed, commitment that moved us into action, and discipline that enabled us to follow through."*
>
> *~ Zig Ziglar*

You must have the discipline to take these steps in advance to prevent the breakdown in the moment when you're pressed for time and don't have healthier alternatives.

I could go on and on with examples, but the determining factor in getting what you want is discipline. More than anything, it's about living your life with conviction and having absolute passion, commitment, and clarity about what you really want.

Attaining Discipline

So how do you get yourself to be disciplined? How do you get yourself to do what you know you need to do? The answer: 100 percent clarity and conviction about what you want in every area of your life and what it means to you. You must attain this, so every single decision you make all day long is executed through that lens. Once you have this clarity and can align every decision to your goal, then your choices are obvious and the discipline to do what you need to do becomes second nature.

The black and white viewpoint that comes with complete clarity lends itself to discipline. Our society does a great job of adding multiple layers of shades of gray. Those who are successful have the strength and conviction to be black and white. You must know there is always a right and wrong answer and decide which will lead you to your goal. Again, it comes back to achieving what you want versus instant gratification. These two things rarely, if ever, align.

What can you do to gain this type of clarity? I understand the sense of overwhelm that can overtake your life, leaving you unable to see the forest for the trees. This is why visualization is incredibly powerful. High achievers visualize daily with clarity and with emotional triggers that remind them to continually make the right choices.

This is not something you can do once, once a year, or even once every few months. Like anything else, it comes down to small daily actions – the daily action of visualization – that continues to build the snowball that ultimately becomes your driving force.

Visualization must be combined with visual tools because these tools are the things that make a difference. Write your goals and post them, so you see them every day. Post of picture of your dream house or boat or car. These create the triggers and cues you need daily. Unless you see them every day, it will be difficult to stay on your path, and those shades of gray will begin taking over and blur the lines of your decision-making process. These visual tools will remind you every day of why you're doing what you're doing and help keep your lens focused on black and white.

Take some time now to write down something that you really want that you haven't been able to achieve or an improvement you want to make:

_____

_____

_____

_____

_____

What two or three daily actions do you need to take to achieve this? I assure you, it's never more than two or three key things that will be the difference maker.

_____

_____

_____

_____

_____

Your higher self is always on the path and acting with intention that allows you to do that which is uncomfortable but necessary to achieve what you truly want. Your lower self tells stories, makes excuses, procrastinates, and feels entitled. No one of us is entitled to anything. It is by our own doing that things either happen or don't happen. We have complete control, and it's critical not to lose sight of that.

How do you live with more discipline to achieve your goal? Again, the answer lies in the visualization and visual tools, the daily rituals you follow, and about consistently returning to your "why." *Why* are you doing what you're doing? Stay focused on what is driving you and the core beliefs you have about your life.

Conversely, if you are super stubborn, you may need to calculate the bad rather than the good. What negative results will occur if you continue to avoid that which you know needs to be done? What will compound negatively over the coming days, weeks, and months if you don't make any changes?

Some people are more driven by negative aversion than positive achievement. If you fall into this category, you need to really understand what negative consequences may befall you, your business, and your family if you fail to take the right actions. If you're in a bad situation, it may become much worse. Perhaps if you fail to take action, you will maintain the status quo and for you, that might be bad enough.

Simplify your life and be disciplined to say "no" to anything that does not serve your family or your higher purpose and goals. I see a lot of people struggle with this: taking on things that don't truly align with their goals and purpose because they're afraid of the conversation to explain why they can't do something or they are simply afraid to say no, create boundries, or draw a line in the sand.

Discipline in Business

There are four specific areas in which you need discipline in your business for unlimited success. I see a lot of lack of discipline in these areas, and it's very clear how that negatively impacts business growth.

These areas are:

- Sales
- Marketing
- Pricing
- People

They aren't the only things that matter, but lacking discipline in these areas is transformationally negative. On the other hand, a high level of discipline in these areas will massively catapult your growth, income, and success beyond what you may imagine to be possible.

When you look at someone who is as successful as you would like to be and wonder what they are have or what they are doing to achieve it, it's not magic or a special characteristic or talent. It's focused discipline in these areas. Even the smartest and most talented people will not be the most successful or even successful at all if they are not applying discipline and doing what needs to be done in these four areas. Discipline in these basic areas is what builds the foundation and allows you to gain momentum.

Take time to look at your basics in these areas and determine what you have been avoiding that has been preventing you from achieving your goals and dreams. Calulate the bad: Where will you be in three, five, or ten years if you stay on the path that you are currently on? Then look at what you want to create for your life and get clear about the steps you need to take to achieve that. Own your choices and decide on your future.

Where have you lacked discipline and how has that affected your personal and professional goals?

_____

_____

What one powerful daily choice or action will you commit to that is going to change your life?

_____

_____

Again, it is small daily actions, done with conviction, that will create the breakthroughs in your life and allow you to achieve the business growth and income that you truly want.

Recap:

> ➤ Discipline is the most powerful characteristic you can have. It allows you to overcome any obstacles you face.

> ➤ Everyone has the power and control to develop self-discipline. It is already inside you.

> ➤ Success and fulfillment aren't derived from whether or not you're good at something. It's about making the decision moment-by-moment that keeps you on your path toward your highest good and the ultimate outcomes you are trying to achieve.

> ➤ Discipline is doing what needs to be done when you don't feel like doing it.

> ➤ Attaining discipline is a matter of being crystal clear about what you want and who you are. With that clarity, being disciplined in your daily decisions becomes second nature.

> ➤ Develop the visualization tools you need to inundate yourself with daily reminders about what you want to achieve. These tools, like clarity, will enable you to make disciplined choices.

➢ Disciplined focus on sales, marketing, pricing, and people in your business is critical for growth and income beyond what you might imagine to be possible.

➢ Small daily actions, done with conviction, create the huge breakthrough.

*Discipline will get you almost anything you want in life. Some people are able to be disciplined independently without input, direction, or management from anyone else. They do very well with self accountability. Others want and need accountability to someone else to stay on track. To get help, visit **KellyRoachCoaching.com/guide** and sign up for the free book guide.*

9

FOCUS ON SOMETHING BIGGER THAN YOURSELF

Success without fulfillment is total and complete failure. As I continued to rise in my career, I had a growing knot in my stomach that this was not life... not the life I wanted. I had immaturely thought that if I achieved the level of income and "success" I wanted, I would be "happy." I was so focused for years on what I wanted to achieve on the exterior that I had ignored what my heart wanted and what my soul needed. Don't make the mistake I did and sacrifice freedom and fulfillment for success. *I'm here to tell you that you can have all three.*

Over the years, I became fiery and passionate about helping people break free of the past, of their current circumstances, and of struggle in their businesses and jobs they hated. I knew with certainty that I had some pretty special gifts and that I had a responsibility to use them to help others succeed. I had hired, trained, and coached hundreds of individuals in a corporate setting and made them successful, but I knew that was not enough.

I knew that the radical growth that I was able to create from 50 to 350 percent year after year for my company would be life changing for small business owners and their families. I also knew that since I had replicated this kind of growth a multitude of times, I certainly could help business owners, entrepreneurs, and other companies do the same.

I spent a full year studying, reading, listening, and learning to everything I could about business, personal growth, Internet marketing, coaching, speaking, and the list goes on. I began to align my exterior life with my interior soul's purpose... and everything became crystal clear to me.

When I launched Kelly Roach Coaching and began consulting and coaching clients nationally and internationally on how to grow their business and achieve their dreams, I knew I had arrived. It was only the beginning, but I was in the right place, using my gifts as God intended.

My purpose on this planet is to help others succeed in a way that allows them to achieve fulfillment, financial abundance, and freedom. While this sounds great in theory, this is not easy to pull off in today's society and culture. People are carrying more responsibility than ever. They are stretched thin, burnt out, and just plain tired.

As a result, many people have simply settled. They stopped dreaming years ago because their current circumstances don't make it easy to pursue their dreams. Our "instant gratification, anything goes" world doesn't reward a lot of the behaviors necessary to achieve true fulfillment in our lives. We are taught to go to school and get a job. Many times, we do not allow ourselves the space to reflect and meditate on what *really* matters. There is a reason why such a large percentage of the population is on anti-depressants and anti-anxiety medications.

Luckily for me, the people who arrive in my programs or hire me to consult with their organization are ready. They want to transform their businesses and their lives, and they are willing to do the work to make it happen. They know it won't be easy but it will be worth it.

These individuals make comments like these:

- I am ready and I am finally doing this, nothing will stop me.
- I know we can make it to the _____dollar mark and I am prepared to do what it takes to make it happen.
- I am done waiting; I am doing this NOW!
- I want to change people's lives and I HAVE to grow my business in order do this.
- I am not putting my dreams on hold any more, let's do this.

But from many others I hear comments like these:

- I know I am standing in my own way.
- I want to pursue my passion, but I can't quit my job.
- I feel like I am just going through the motions, running from one thing to the next.
- I am a prisoner in my own life; there is no time or space for my goals, dreams or aspirations.
- I am not doing what I really want to do, but I need to pay the bills somehow.
- I have tried everything and I just can't breakthrough.
- *Have you ever felt these things or made comments like these?*

Which of these two series of comments sounds more like you?

When I am helping people create radical change in their businesses and lives, I always tell them to get out of their own head and focus on something bigger than themselves. When you stop being so focused on yourself and begin to shift your focus to the difference you can make, the people you can help, that will create the passion that will pull you.

I literally have a never-ending stream of passion, excitement, and dedication to growing my business because every client I take on is a life I can change. It's not about me; it's about them. I have to focus on growing my mission, visibility, and impact so that I can help as many people as possible.

Your mental attitude and perspective determine all of your results and shape your life experience. The greatest gift you can give yourself is to focus on something bigger than yourself. The biggest pitfall I see with individuals who want something different or more in their lives but are struggling to make real headway in getting it is that they are stuck in their own heads. Imperfect action with intention daily is the only way to make your dreams come true.

This means getting over yourself and valuing the result and end game more than you fear rejection, being judged, and the possibility of failure.

Nine out of ten people you meet are not living a life that in any way resembles their goals, dreams, or passions in life. It is much easier to limp along getting by than it is to make the radical changes necessary to achieve something extraordinary in your life. But does this mean it's not worth it?

Let me repeat a critical concept:

It's about living your life now like no one else will, so you can live your life later like no one else can.

It always amazes me that people will go about living their whole life unfulfilled and dissatisfied rather than spending a few years in sacrifice to achieve a lifetime of positive results. This is why you need to take very specific steps to put yourself in the flow and on the path to where you want to be.

On my own journey, I have realized there are five critical components to set yourself up on a no-fail plan to overcome the obstacles that come along and achieve at a level that very few ever do:

1. Inner drive, work ethic, focus on something bigger than yourself
2. Coaching or mentoring
3. Masterminding
4. Community
5. Education, resources, information, and inspiration

After experiencing many different programs myself and working for years to perfect the ultimate way to help people achieve greatness, these are the five components I have found will give you the critical edge needed to achieve results beyond belief.

You have to bring the first one; everything else you can seek outside of yourself to get the support you need to succeed. All of my programs are designed to ensure all of these needs are met, so individuals who are committed are given the absolute best chance at success.

So let's talk about how each of these five will catapult you to a level you could not achieve otherwise.

Inner Drive, Work Ethic, and Focusing on Something Bigger than Yourself.

There are no short cuts. It will never get easier and nothing of great value is achieved without true and diligent effort over time.

Operating every day with a value system including integrity, work ethic, diligence, and a genuine interest in helping others will never steer you wrong. It is the inner burning fire, the clarity around your *why*, that thing that is bigger than you that will keep you going when times get tough. Creating visuals like a dream board and doing daily rituals such as meditation and journaling will help you stay the course even when you are dying for the instant gratification that you are not getting.

Coaching or Mentoring

Everyone that you see performing at the top of their field has someone in their corner advising them, guiding them, and preventing them from making devastating mistakes. Many people have the misperception that the time to get a coach is once you are successful. Quite the contrary is true: The most important time to have a coach is when you are on the way up. It will literally cut years off your timeline for success. It did for me, and I do this for my clients each and every day. Can you imagine a professional athlete never working with a coach until they got to the pro level? It's never happened, of course, because you need a coach to get there.

The best way to think of a coach is that you are dropped in the middle of the jungle at midnight without a flashlight or a clue as to where you are. A coach is the experienced woodsman with a flashlight and an encyclopedic knowledge of how to cross the treacherous jungle safely in the fastest, most efficient way possible.

> *Napoleon Hill wrote about the* **mastermind group** *principle as: "The coordination of knowledge and effort of two or more people, who work toward a definite purpose, in the spirit of harmony."*

You need to choose your coach or mentor wisely though. Just because they are in the business you want to be in or have done it for a certain number of years means nothing. Evaluate them based on their accomplishments and level of achievement in the area you want to excel in *and* if their heart is in it! At a certain point, someone may have the talent, capability, and level of accomplishment but no longer has the passion or fire for themselves… let alone to help someone else. This is not the type of person to whom you want to entrust your success.

Give yourself the best chance possible by finding a mentor who is deeply invested in helping people like you and does it with joy, lovingly not just for the money.

Masterminding

Many times, when given the opportunity to work with a coach or get laser coaching (short 15-20 minute sessions), you won't even know where to begin. You can get so lost in everything you need to do that you need prompting and perspective to understand where to focus. I cannot say enough about the power of masterminding to accelerate the results you are getting.

Whether you need resources, introductions, referrals or joint partners, direction, information, or collaboration, putting yourself in the right mastermind can do all of this and more for you.

A mastermind also gives you the opportunity to get pre-launch feedback and prevent mistakes that you would not even recognize because you are so "in your own head."

The right mastermind also keeps you moving and accountable because you are in the mix with doers, action takers, and individuals pushing their own limits every day.

Community

As you decide to commit to the future you really want, a lot will change in your life. You will no longer want to be around people who are toxic to your growth or who don't support the goals you are trying to achieve.

You will have less tolerance of the B.S. from the people around you who aren't doing anything with their lives besides complaining and will instead surround yourself with positive, motivated individuals who can provide a support system for you.

Community is critical as you progress through the various stages of achieving greatness in your life. As I always say, "All hell breaks loose when you decide you are really ready to make it happen." As soon as you commit to something really big for yourself, you will notice problems, challenges, and turbulence creep up from all angles. It will be tempting to quit... often. Community is what keeps you going during those tough times, helps you remember your *why*, and keeps you going even when it feels borderline impossible.

Education, Resources, Information and Inspiration

These things are *critical* you your success. No one knows everything they need to know to get from where they are to where they need to be. Although we innately have the ability, we do need the right education, tools, and resources to move through each stage of accomplishing our goals.

Whatever areas you decide to focus your energy on to achieve the principles discussed in this book, make sure you assess your own knowledge and get support accordingly. Going at it alone is the biggest mistake anyone can make in trying to achieve something extraordinary.

With Google, YouTube, and all of the free information on the Internet today, you can learn almost anything for only the cost of your time. Those who are resourceful win, period.

In addition to the Internet, there are programs that coaches and consultants like myself offer in almost every topic under the sun to give you the information, education, and resources you need to succeed.

Again, let someone who has successfully done the thing that you want to do layout an exact roadmap for you to follow instead of trying to go at it alone without a clue; it's totally unnecessary. It will cost you more in mistakes than it will to get help.

What's Your Epitaph?

Finally, look at your life from your final day on the planet. Start with the end in mind. Make decisions from the long view, not a "short-term, I want it now" mentality.

Ask yourself: "What would my gravestone read if I died today?" Are you happy with the legacy you would leave if this were the end of the story, not the beginning?

Chances are when you begin thinking this way you will make decisions differently. There is also a strong possibility that the changes you want to make are not only for yourself, but also for the people you love, the planet, and community you serve.

Start living this way today. None of us knows how long we have, so make it count today.

Live life with no regrets. Say what you really feel, love the way you want to be loved, and use your gifts and potential in the way that deep down you know in your heart and soul were intended.

Focus on something bigger than yourself and you will have the confidence to overcome great adversity and become numb to judgment and the fear of failure.

It's time to step into your greatness and let your light shine.

Recap:

➢ It isn't all about success. In fact, failure can be defined as success without fulfillment. Don't fail.

➢ When you align your exterior life with your interior soul's purpose, everything will become crystal clear.

➢ You must allow yourself the space and time to reflect and meditate on what *really* matters.

➢ There are five critical areas that will help you create a no-fail plan for success:

✓ Inner drive, work ethic, focus on something bigger than yourself
✓ Coaching or mentoring
✓ Masterminding
✓ Community
✓ Education, resources, information, and inspiration

➢ Start living today in such a way that it will write the epitaph you desire and create the legacy you want to leave.

You can't help others, impact the world, create a movement, and more if your tank is empty. A great way to focus on giving back is to focus on your own personal growth and then share what you have learned with others. Listening to podcasts and reading books like this can help you accelerate your growth and maximize your ability to achieve your goals.

If you haven't done so already, start tuning in to Unstoppable Success Radio each week to stretch your mind and reinvigorate your spirit. The show is hosted on both iTune and Sticher™.

Now Is Your Time to Thrive

If you made it this far either you are *truly* committed to changing your life and creating a better future for yourself and your family... or you cheated and skipped to the finale.

If you cheated and skipped right to this point, I'll suggest to you – no, I'll tell you straight out – you have cheated yourself. There are no shortcuts. There is no silver bullet to success, no magic pill you can swallow and have it all be as you want it to be. (So head on back to Chapter 1)!

As I have been stressing throughout the book, success comes primarily from daily, imperfect action. If the road to hell is paved with a thousand good intentions, the road to success is paved with thousands of small, intentional, and clearly directed actions. I want you to be on the road to success, but the choice is yours and yours alone.

I want you to leave with the deep confidence, conviction and certainty that **you can** achieve all of your goals and dreams if you are willing to **take action, stay committed and follow through on the simple, powerful keys discussed in this book.**

You now have the roadmap, insights, and strategies I used and hundreds of others are using to grow their business, achieve freedom, and live their dreams.

Let's run through the nine principles one more time to bring it all together:

1. Stop resenting the 1% and join them: If you are willing to do the work, educate yourself, and not quit when the going gets tough, you can become or achieve anything you desire.

2. Cultivate an entrepreneurial spirit: With an entrepreneurial spirit, you question everything, are intentional about every component of your life, make bold and empowered decisions, and you alone determine your worth.

3. Act like a CEO if you want to earn like one: Success doesn't occur in one grand moment; it results from the daily decisions you make, and yes, there will be sacrifices along the way.

4. Leadership: Your ability to create freedom is directly proportionate to your ability to impact and influence others – the essence of leadership.

5. Business mastery: Unless you are willing to hustle and stop simply showing up and clocking in, nothing will change. You must be the one to shake things up and set things on fire in order to achieve what you want in life.

6. Invest in yourself daily: You have free will; therefore, you have the ability to change your life and get started on a new path.

7. Sales: Success depends on sales, and sales is not simply a monetary transfer for the goods and services you provide. It is the transfer of inspiration to get others to do what you want them to do for their own reasons.

8. Discipline: Discipline is doing what needs to be done when you don't feel like doing it.

9. Focus on something bigger than yourself: Start living today in such a way that it will write the epitaph you desire and create the legacy you want to leave.

The bottom line is that you need to connect your daily actions with the outcomes you are trying to achieve. This means your thoughts, behaviors, and decisions must reflect your goals... *daily*.

You may need to wake up early, stay up late, do things that scare you, and take risks that make you uncomfortable. The bottom line is: There are no short cuts to success. You have to be willing to do the work and follow through no matter how challenging it may sometimes seem.

The truth is there are certain things that almost all highly successful people have in common. If you begin embodying these things chances are you will be too:

- Put yourself in a supportive, positive community of like-minded people who are further along than you are.
- Get coaching, mentoring, and support from someone who has achieved what you hope to one day.
- Take care of your mind, body, and soul – every area of life is interconnected. You have to be full in order to deliver and give to others.
- Remove toxic people, habits, and things that distract you from forward progress.
- Work tirelessly to strengthen your resilience, muscle, your mental toughness to help you weather the storms in business and in life.
- Live with love, integrity, honesty, and passion.

Remember that every overnight success was years in the making and every one you look up to was one day exactly where you are now. You can do this!

So now it's your turn to set a new standard for your business and life.

What changes will you make immediately that will create more freedom, financial abundance and fulfillment in your life?

_____

_____

What has held you back up until now that you will no longer let stand in your way?

_____

_____

What support do you need to accomplish your goals? What will you do right away to ensure you have the right tools, resources, training and mentoring to get to your goals?

_____

_____

Accountability is the key to achieving your goals. Being in the company of like-minded, success-driven individuals who are serious about achieving the next level of success will push you to step up your game and stay focused until you achieve your dreams. Visit KellyRoachCoaching.com/guide and sign up for the free book guide that will take you from motivation to action. This book is not meant to just be read; it is meant to be acted upon. This free guide will help you do just that.

At the end of the day, **unstoppable success** comes down to a mindset of optimism, determination, and continuous strategic action. Start building your snowball of unstoppable success one action at a time, one day at a time.

When you believe in yourself and commit to your why, nothing can stop you.

Now go set the world on fire!

DOWNLOAD THE FREE GUIDE

There are a bunch of resources that can help you take this information and these strategies and implement them into your own life.

To help you do just that, I put together a free book guide that you can use to start getting the clarity you need on your own business and life.

Take step 1, and download these free resources by visiting:

KellyRoachCoaching.com/guide

ABOUT THE AUTHOR

Kelly Roach has helped hundreds of individuals master sales, marketing, and business growth strategy to grow their incomes and achieve their goals.

Kelly started her career with a Fortune 500 firm where she was promoted seven times in eight years, becoming the youngest Senior Vice President in the firm. Kelly's experience hiring, training, coaching, and managing individuals across 17 locations up and down the East Coast prepared her for her entrepreneurial journey.

After breaking every record in the company's history for profit, growth, sales, and expansion, coupled with millions in profit added to the bottom line, Kelly knew it was time to focus on helping others do the same.

Kelly's number one passion in life is helping others succeed in business and life with the right strategies, action plan, and mindset for success. Kelly's company, **Kelly Roach Coaching** helps entrepreneurs, business owners and executive leaders achieve rapid, sustainable business growth in record time. You can learn more about who Kelly is and how she helps people at www.kellyroachcoaching.com.

Kelly does private consulting with corporations, runs online training and coaching programs for entrepreneurs, and hosts her own Elite Mastermind for individuals who are seriously committed to transformative results in their business and life.

Kelly frequently does media appearances and speaking engagements in addition to being the CEO at Kelly Roach Coaching and hosting her weekly podcast, "Unstoppable Success Radio." Visit iTunes or Sticher^{TM} radio to tune in weekly to gain invaluable insights, strategies, resources and more at:

Unstoppable Success Radio:

On iTunes: www.KellyRoachCoaching.com/iTunes

On Sticher™: www.KellyRoachCoaching.com/stitcher

Kelly, her husband, Billy, and daughter, Madison, live in West Chester, Pennsylvania with their two beagles, Sadie and Macy.

Now known internationally as the "Authority for Entrepreneurs and Business Leaders who want more success, freedom, and fulfillment in their lives," Kelly is on a mission to help 1,000,000 people achieve their goals and dreams.

Connect with Kelly:

Facebook: www.facebook.com/kellyroachinternational

LinkedIn: www.linkedin.com/in/kellyovertonroach

Twitter: @kellyroachint

To learn how you can work with Kelly and her team, email coaching@kellyroachcoaching.com or visit www.kellyroachcoaching. com to get in touch with us today.

To order this book as a key resource for an event, seminar, or gifts for clients simply email customersupport@kellyroachcoaching. com to learn more.

HIRE KELLY TO SPEAK

Kelly speaks nationally and internationally on topics related to entrepreneurial success, leadership, sales mastery, the power of mindset, and how to create unstoppable success in business and in life.

As a former NFL cheerleader turned Fortune 500 executive now Million-Dollar Marketing Mentor, Kelly brings a level of energy, clarity and passion to the stage that you will be hard pressed to find elsewhere.

To learn more about booking Kelly for conferences, panels, and team leadership meetings and retreats visit www.kellyroachcoaching.com/speaking or email speaking@kellyroachcoaching.com.

Here are what people are saying about Kelly:

"Unforgettable Content and Actionable Growth Strategies"

"Kelly Roach is not only a powerhouse Business Growth Strategist, she is a phenomenal speaker and coach. Sure to engage and inspire your audience, Kelly brings experience and a proven track record to the presentations she delivers. Whether you are asking her to speak to a group of five or 5,000, Kelly delivers unforgettable content and actionable growth strategies in a simple, yet powerful way. I highly recommend Kelly the next time you need a speaker to truly WOW your audience."

- Angela V. Megasko,
President & CEO Market Viewpoint LLC

"My audience was literally mesmerized!"

"Kelly Roach is a phenomenal speaker! I could end there and that would be enough, but I'll share more! Kelly spoke at my sold-out event, Dream Business Academy, on the topic of sales, and she knocked it out of the park! My audience was literally mesmerized as she shared her story and the action steps she uses in her business, and teaches her students, on how to turn warm leads into $100K in six months or less. It is rare to have a speaker openly and willingly share so much of the 'good stuff' in a setting like that!"

- Jim Palmer,
Author, Speaker, Entrepreneur, Coach

"Kelly Roach is THE Business Growth Coach"

"From the moment Kelly hits the stage, she fills the room with energy, enthusiasm, and a level of expertise any organization or conference would be lucky to have. Kelly Roach is THE Business Growth Coach for those who are serious about creating record breaking results in minimal time."

- Dr. Joanny Lui,
Author of Knock OUT Concussions and Heal Your Concussion

"Refreshing and Dynamic"

"Kelly Roach is so refreshing and dynamic with her presentation. Kelly's to-the-point speaking, along with great business-building advice, has created a vital approach to growing any business to a level that soars above the rest."

- Dr. Raynette C. Ilg N.D.

HIRE KELLY TO HELP YOU TRANSFORM YOUR BUSINESS

Kelly works with clients nationally and internationally in a variety of capacities as a speaker, consultant and coach.

Kelly's core focus areas include:

- **How to design, launch and build your 7-figure business foundation**
- **Rapid, sustainable growth strategies**
- **How to design and build a winning team**
- **Impactful and influential leadership**
- **Sales and marketing strategy and implementation**
- **Organizational development and growth planning**

You can email Kelly's team directly at <u>customersupport@ kellyroachcoaching.com</u> to learn more about all of Kelly's products and services.

To join Kelly's exclusive email communities and to be the first to receive her trainings, resources, videos and more, visit <u>www.kellyroachcoaching.com</u>.

ACKNOWLEDGEMENTS

I have been blessed with many people coming in and out of my life for various reasons and seasons who have impacted me in profound ways. There are too many to mention, so I will not try to cover them all, but there are a few that I would like to touch on.

First and foremost, I am thankful to my parents for raising me to believe in myself, live a life of integrity, and to always be the best I can possibly be. My husband, Billy, who has supported me in countless ways, and my daughter, Madison, who inspires me endlessly.

I have had many incredible business coaches, mentors, and colleagues from whom I have learned so much, and I am eternally grateful. My mentor for the past 11 years, Dave, quite literally changed the trajectory of my life – thank you. Thank you to Joyce Crane who taught me to be tough, disciplined, and fight for my dreams no matter what.

Without my sister, Melanie, this business would not have achieved the massive growth and success that is has over the past few years. Thank you for supporting me, believing in me, and working so hard to help me bring my work to the world.

Austin at Epic Launch: You are the kind of person every entrepreneur dreams of partnering with on a project like this. Thank you for going above and beyond to make this book happen. Jim Palmer: Thank you for pushing me to write this book and to share this work with the people who can benefit from it.

To my clients: I cannot even begin to express my gratitude to you. It is an honor to be able to serve you as you build your businesses and achieve your dreams.

~ Kelly Roach

ONE LAST THING

May I ask you for a favor?

If you got anything out of this book, whether it inspired you or taught you anything at all, I would forever be grateful if you did something small for me...

Will you please give a copy of this book to a friend, family member or colleague?

Ask them to read it. Let them know what's possible for them if they start to value their dreams and implement some of the principles discussed in this book.

Let them know they can become UNSTOPPABLE.

We need them. We need you. Please spread the word.

Thank you yet again,

~ Kelly Roach